Short Bike Rides®
in Connecticut

Help Us Keep This Guide Up to Date

Every effort has been made by the author and editors to make this guide as accurate and useful as possible. However, many things can change after a guide is published–establishments close, phone numbers change, hiking trails are rerouted, facilities come under new management, etc.

We would love to hear from you concerning your experiences with this guide and how you feel it could be made better and be kept up to date. While we may not be able to respond to all comments and suggestions, we'll take them to heart and we'll also make certain to share them with the author. Please send your comments and suggestions to the following address:

The Globe Pequot Press
Reader Response/Editorial Department
P.O. Box 480
Guilford, CT 06437

Or you may e-mail us at:

editorial@globe-pequot.com

Thanks for your input, and happy travels!

Short Bike Rides® Series

Short Bike Rides®
in
Connecticut

Sixth Edition

by

Edwin Mullen *and* Jane Griffith

Guilford, Connecticut

Photographs on pages viii, 4, 16, 20, 84, 120 by Henry Hosley; page 12 from the State of Connecticut Department of Commerce; Pages 32, 44, 48, 52, 60, 68, 92, 112 by Laurent Mullen; page 104 by Lisabeth Huck; all others by Edwin Mullen.

Library of Congress Cataloging-in-Publication Data

Mullen, Edwin.
  Short bike rides in Connecticut / by Edwin Mullen and Jane Griffith. — 6th ed.
        p.   cm. — (Short bike rides series)
    ISBN 0-7627-0205-2
    1. Bicycle touring—Connecticut—Guidebooks. 2. Connecticut—Guidebooks.   I. Griffith, Jane, 1934–   II. Title.   III. Series.
    GV1045.5.C66G75 1998
    917.4604'43—dc21   97-46432
                                                           CIP

Manufactured in the United States of America
Second Edition/Fourth Printing

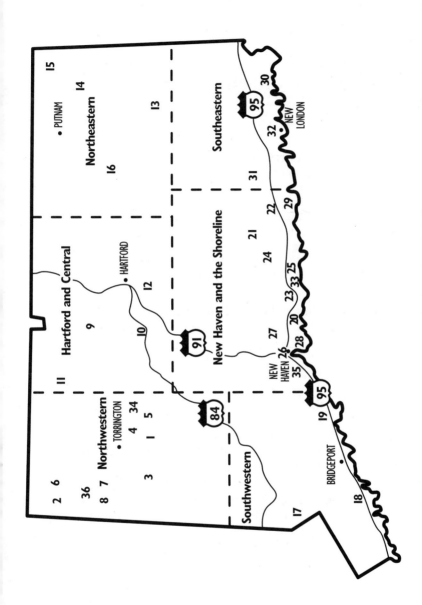

Table of Contents

New Haven and the Shoreline

Southeastern Connecticut

Combination Rides

Introduction

This book combines two unique and pleasurable experiences—riding a bicycle and exploring Connecticut, the exquisite little state the Algonquin Indians called the "place of the long river." That river is the Connecticut, which flows for 407 miles from northern New Hampshire across Massachusetts and Connecticut into Long Island Sound. It would be a short river in the Midwest, but in Connecticut, the third smallest state, it's a long river, wide and deep, with relatively little industry or urban sprawl marring its banks.

Connecticut has everything: forests and mountains with whitewater rivers, farms and streams, village greens, lakes, saltwater beaches, and historic houses from the eighteenth century in every town and village and several from the seventeenth. The Guilford ride will lead you to the oldest stone house in America, the beautifully preserved Henry Whitfield house, which dates to 1639. It's a small museum, and there are many more museums, large and small: Mystic Seaport, with more than 350 years of Connecticut's heritage and tradition on working display in ships and shops of the eighteenth and nineteenth centuries; Farmington's Hillstead Museum; the Aldrich in Ridgefield, with its fabulous outdoor sculpture; and the traveling museum of the Valley Railroad Company in Essex, which takes you for an hour-long ride on a lovingly restored steam train up to Deep River, where you can embark on an authentic riverboat for a closer look at the Connecticut River and its shores. All of these museums are located along one of our bike rides.

Although it's one of the original thirteen states, Connecticut remains 90 percent woodland, and as you ride through its woodlands or along its shores, you see everything around you, taking in the full beauty of the sights and sounds and scents of the countryside. When you stop to rest and reflect with a quiet picnic beside a small lake or stream, you'll know that the pure joy of bicycles is much more than pedaling.

To get the most out of this book, plan a vacation around it—a four-day weekend or a full week at one of the fine old country inns that grace the Connecticut countryside. They're all in *Recommended Country Inns® of New England* by Elizabeth Squier. Choose the area—mountains, flatlands, or shoreline—pick an inn, and, of course, bring your bicycles!

To ensure your enjoyment, follow the precautions outlined in the section on safety and take along some good equipment. For picnics and swimming, pannier and handlebar bags are indispensable. As for the bike itself, I now recommend the twenty-one speed hybrid mountain/road bike that has fat and deep tread tires but a lighter frame than its mountain cousin. It doesn't track as well as the touring bike; but for seeing the countryside, it has a more upright posture; and for the occasional dirt road or sudden swerve onto grass or dirt shoulder, it's hard to beat. The extra gears combined with the latest shifters with their positive response are marvelous!

Now that you're ready to start out, I'd like to thank you for buying my book on exploring beautiful Connecticut, and I'd like to invite you to write me with your comments, complaints, suggestions, observations—whatever you like. Write to me, Edwin Mullen, c/o The Globe Pequot Press, P. O. Box 833, Old Saybrook, CT 06475.

Godspeed—and may the wind be always at your back!

Safety

Riding the roads of Connecticut on a bicycle is one of life's rewarding pleasures, but it *can* be dangerous. Some of the rides (i.e., numbers 9, Avon-Simsbury; 17, Ridgefield; and 32, Waterford-New London) include sections that traverse heavily traveled roads, especially on weekdays. If you cannot do these on a weekend, it is advisable to check them out in your car first. Observe all Connecticut state vehicle laws plus those unique to the bicycle: ride with traffic, staying close to the right; give clear hand signals; yield to pedestrians; ride single file; walk your bike on sidewalks in town centers.

Stop at red lights and stop signs. Ride defensively. Be wary of motorists—all of them! They probably don't see you, and a fender-bender to them is a leg-breaker or worse to you. Be visible at night and wear a helmet—doing so reduces your risk of serious injury in an accident by 75 percent. Check your bike before beginning a trip; make sure that all nuts are tight and the derailleurs and brakes are working properly; take a spare tube, a set of plastic tire levers, an air pump, and an adjustable wrench. Here's a helpful checklist:

1. Brakes
2. Derailleurs and chain
3. Wheels
4. Tires
5. Helmet and gloves
6. Rearview mirror
7 Reflectors
8. Tool kit
9. Small first aid kit
10. Bolt-cutter-proof lock
11. Wash 'n Dri towelettes
12. Pannier and handlebar bags
13. Water bottle
14. Reflective vest
15. Sunglasses
16. Insect repellent
17. Food
18. Picnic ground cloth
19. Bathing suit
20. Towel
21. Watch
22. *Short Bike Rides in Connecticut*

Bantam Lake

Number of miles:	10
Approximate pedaling time:	1½ hours
Terrain:	quite hilly on the east side of the lake, otherwise undemanding
Surface:	good
Things to see:	Point Folly Camp Ground, Bantam Lake, Litchfield Nature Center, Sandy Beach

Bantam Lake, the largest natural lake in Connecticut, encircled by a country road and replete with an uncrowded sandy beach, the 4,000 acres of forest in the state's largest nature center and wildlife sanctuary, the White Memorial Foundation, is a jewel of a ride! It starts from the foundation's parking lot at the end of the entrance road—a ½-mile-long, hard-packed dirt road off Bissell Road. When you are ready, ride back to Bissell Road, turn left and left again onto Route 202 to North Shore Road, which is on the left across from the sign WAMOGO REGIONAL HIGH SCHOOL.

North Shore Road skirts the end of the lake, winding through an area of modest cottages, swinging to the right, and up a steep, short hill to Route 209. Turn left and in about a mile notice the peninsula of Deer Isle. You will pass several restaurants and places to rent boats. About 4 miles into the ride, you'll arrive at the lake's southern end. Start uphill. At the junction of Routes 209 and 109, turn left and continue uphill. Just after reaching the crest of the hill, you'll spot East Shore Road on the left; turn here. At the top of your next climb, the road levels off and you'll want to stop to take in the view of the lake. Continue along East Shore Road to Sandy Beach, which is open to the

Bantam Lake

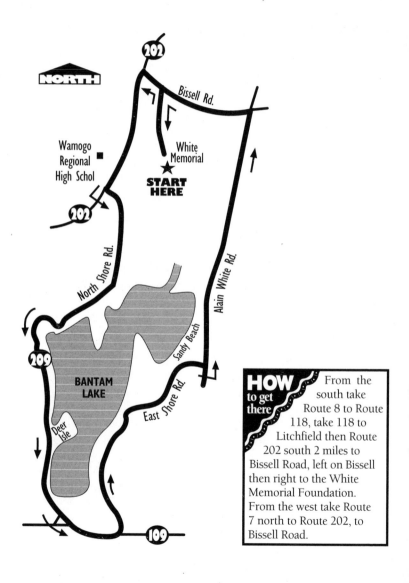

NORTH

Wamogo Regional High Schol

202

Bissell Rd.

White Memorial

START HERE

202

North Shore Rd.

Alain White Rd.

Sandy Beach

209

BANTAM LAKE

East Shore Rd.

Deer Isle

109

HOW to get there From the south take Route 8 to Route 118, take 118 to Litchfield then Route 202 south 2 miles to Bissell Road, left on Bissell then right to the White Memorial Foundation. From the west take Route 7 north to Route 202, to Bissell Road.

public on Memorial Day weekend, weekends only in June, and then starting July 1 through Labor Day, seven days a week, 9:00 A.M. to 7:00 P.M. There's a $1.00 fee to park your bike. Next continue about a mile to where East Shore Road comes to a T at Alain White Road; turn left. Approximately 8½ miles into the ride, turn left onto Bissell Road. You are now on a wide paved road leading through the majestic forest of the 4,000-acre White Memorial, which was created by Alain and Mary White, whose parents established a summer residence in Litchfield in 1863. Alain and Mary purchased 4,000 acres around Bantam Lake between 1908 and 1912, and in 1913, in memory of their parents, they founded a nonprofit trust to provide a sanctuary for conservation, passive recreation, a nature center, and museum for education and research, all of which exist to this day.

After about 1 mile, turn left into the grounds of the White Memorial Nature Center and Museum.

In ½ mile you'll arrive at the headquarters of White Memorial. Here you'll find a large outdoor map of the center's 35 miles of trails; the Nature Center and Museum, with exhibits and restrooms; and many lovely sites for picnicking. Many of the 35 miles of trails are available for bike riding. They are marked, as the foot trails are not open to bikes.

The Museum has been extensively refurbished and is worth visiting. Admission is $2.00.

Lakeville–Sharon

Number of miles:	14
Approximate pedaling time:	2 hours
Terrain:	hilly
Surface:	good
Things to see:	Salisbury, Lake Wononscopomuc, Lakeville, Hotchkiss School, Mudge Pond, Sharon

Lakeville–Sharon is up in Connecticut's mountain country where the Berkshires, respecting no human boundaries, stride majestically through New York, Massachusetts, and Connecticut. It's one of four rides up here: Salisbury–Falls Village, West Cornwall–Furnace Creek, West Cornwall–Lime Rock, and Lakeville–Sharon. All take you through the valleys, across the rivers, around the mountains, and up *some* hills, so it does help to be in good shape when you come up here. Do come—the scenery is spectacular. Stay at an inn and ride them all. Try White Hart Inn in Salisbury, The Inn On Lake Waramaug, or Boulders Inn, also on the shore of Lake Waramaug—or camp at Lake Waramaug State Park.

Park your car on Main Street in Lakeville. Head west on Route 44, which takes you up and down short hills that follow the shape of Lake Wononscopomuc. In 1 mile at the top of a hill, you will come to a fork; bear left. You are now on Indian Mountain Road. Soon you will have a ½-mile-long downhill. At the bottom of it there is a four-way stop sign, where Route 112 crosses your street. When you get to the top of the next ridge, you have a wonderful view of neighboring valleys and hillsides. Soon there is a mile-long downhill sweep, then the road levels off, narrows, and comes to a T almost imperceptibly at

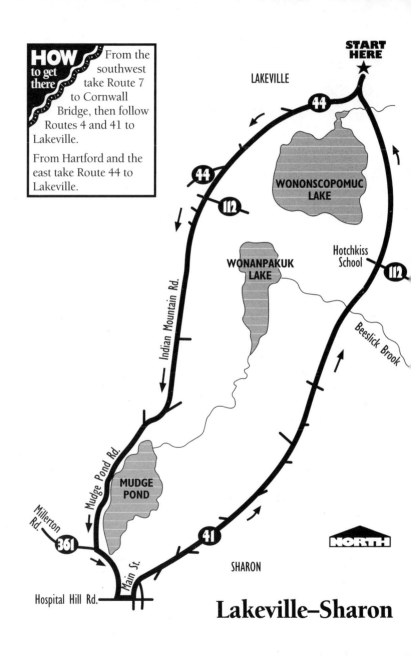

HOW to get there
From the southwest take Route 7 to Cornwall Bridge, then follow Routes 4 and 41 to Lakeville.

From Hartford and the east take Route 44 to Lakeville.

START HERE

LAKEVILLE

44

112

WONONSCOPOMUC LAKE

WONANPAKUK LAKE

Hotchkiss School

112

Beeslick Brook

Indian Mountain Rd.

Mudge Pond Rd.

MUDGE POND

Millerton Rd.

361

Main St.

Hospital Hill Rd.

SHARON

NORTH

Lakeville–Sharon

Mudge Road, which comes in from your left and promptly changes its name to Mudge Pond Road. The road makes a sharp right turn and then a sharp left as it nears the pond. After you pass the Sharon town beach (residents only, alas), you'll find several beautiful sites for a picnic on the border of the lake.

The route along the pond is about $1\frac{1}{2}$ miles long. Then comes a steep uphill, which takes you out of the valley and yields an expansive view of it. Now the road goes down and comes to a T at Millerton Road (Route 361). Turn left toward the town of Sharon. Just before the town, the road climbs steeply past a cemetery on the left and then comes to a T at West Main Street at the Sharon Green. Turn left to explore the village and then turn north on Main Street (Route 41). Route 41 goes uphill out of town. From the crest you can see some of the state's finest scenery. You are skirting a ridge here, going uphill gently at first, then more steeply for $\frac{3}{10}$ mile, and finally going downhill for $\frac{1}{2}$ mile. This is followed by a long, gradual incline. At the crest take a break to enjoy the panoramic vista that rolls down the valley and across farm after farm to the western horizon—a rare and breathtaking sight. You have earned it. En route again, another long hill takes you to the junction with Route 112. Here ride through the grounds of Hotchkiss School if you like, then continue north on Route 41, enjoying the remaining 2 miles of the ride, which are generally downhill.

Lake Waramaug

Number of miles:	8
Approximate pedaling time:	1¼ hours
Terrain:	flat
Surface:	good
Things to see:	the lake itself, Boulders Inn, The Inn on Lake Waramaug, Hopkins Vineyard Winery, Lake Waramaug State Park

Lake Waramaug has everything for a long, happy, and relaxed weekend. The state park at the western end of the lake has been much improved and made more beautiful over the twenty-one years since Jane Griffith and I first created the ride. Today, the beach and picnic area have been enlarged to where there are dozens of picnic sites along the shore of the lake and more camping sites, parking is still free, and there are changing rooms as well as rest rooms! So saddle up and from the park head out to the right, counterclockwise around the lake. The route is relatively flat and affords fine views of the lake, a large one set down at the base of surrounding hills, which are covered with magnificent foliage, especially in the fall.

After 4 miles of easy riding along the shore of the lake, you will come to the southern end, where there is a commercial boat-launching area, a restaurant, and a beer parlor as well as a town beach. Next is a short uphill stretch on Route 45, leveling off near the Boulders Inn, which offers lodging and dining and has a fine view of the lake. In less than ½ mile you'll come to North Shore Road; turn left, leaving Route 45, and continue your circuit. North Shore Road is a tiny, narrow road that twists and turns, following the natural contours of the shoreline.

Lake Waramaug

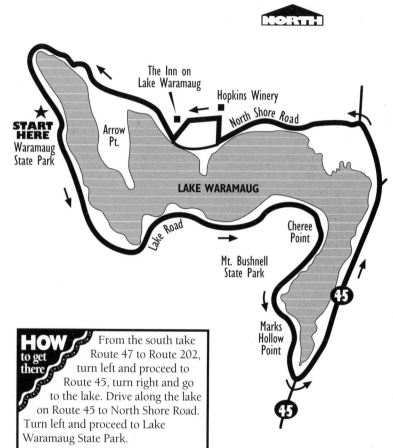

NORTH

The Inn on
Lake Waramaug

Hopkins Winery

North Shore Road

★ START HERE
Waramaug
State Park

Arrow
Pt.

LAKE WARAMAUG

Lake Road

Cheree
Point

Mt. Bushnell
State Park

Marks
Hollow
Point

45

45

HOW to get there From the south take
Route 47 to Route 202,
turn left and proceed to
Route 45, turn right and go
to the lake. Drive along the lake
on Route 45 to North Shore Road.
Turn left and proceed to Lake
Waramaug State Park.

From the northeast take Route 44
west to Route 202 through
Torrington and Litchfield to Route
45, then proceed as above.

On this stretch you'll come to the Hopkins Inn and Hopkins Vineyard Winery. Turn right and go up a short, steep hill to the winery, which is well worth a stop! The Hopkins family has been farming on this land since 1787. They planted twenty acres of vineyards in 1979, opened their winery in 1981, and are happy to have you taste their fine whites and reds free of charge.

After your visit, turn right and continue along the hillside for a short distance, until you turn ninety degrees left and rejoin North Shore Road. Turn right on North Shore Road. Soon you'll see The Inn on Lake Waramaug. This fine old inn, set on a hillside overlooking the lake, has property on the lake front, where there are sailboats and swimming and picnicking for the guests.

As you continue on North Shore Road, you will be struck by the fact that long stretches of the shoreline have not been developed. Fields go right down to the water's edge in some places. This is one of the few lakes we have seen that is not entirely taken over by signs saying PRIVATE, KEEP OUT, so riding here is particularly unhurried, unharried, and joyful. Around the next bend you will be able to see the state park. When you come to the entrance, turn left and you are back at your starting place.

We first took this ride in October (when the woods were wild with color), and as we rounded the bend into the park, we came upon two cyclist-campers taking a swim after putting up their tent and making camp. As we loaded our bikes for the trip home, we vowed to come back and camp there the following summer.

Litchfield

Number of miles:	4
Approximate pedaling time:	1 hour
Terrain:	flat in town, two hills getting in and out
Surface:	good
Things to see:	Litchfield itself, with its eighteenth-century houses, the country's first law school, Litchfield Historical Museum, the eighteenth-century Congregational church

Litchfield is a short *Short Bike Ride* designed to give you a leisurely look at this quintessential New England village of the mid-seventeen hundreds. It is best to arrive between 10:00 A.M. and 4:00 P.M. on any day except Sunday, so you can visit the Litchfield Historical Museum located on the corner of South and East streets before you start out on the ride. It has displays in its four galleries and an outstanding manuscript collection of old Litchfield. A note on parking your motorized vehicle: The town of Litchfield has instituted one- and two-hour limits for parking around the small green, so I suggest that you park behind one of the nearby churches.

Start from the Litchfield Green. At the east end of the green, turn right onto South Street (Route 63). Just around the corner there is an entrance into Cobble Court, an old cobblestone courtyard bordered with fascinating shops. Continue down South Street, which is flanked on both sides by eighteenth-century homes, one of which housed the first law school in America, started in 1775 by Tapping Reeves, whose

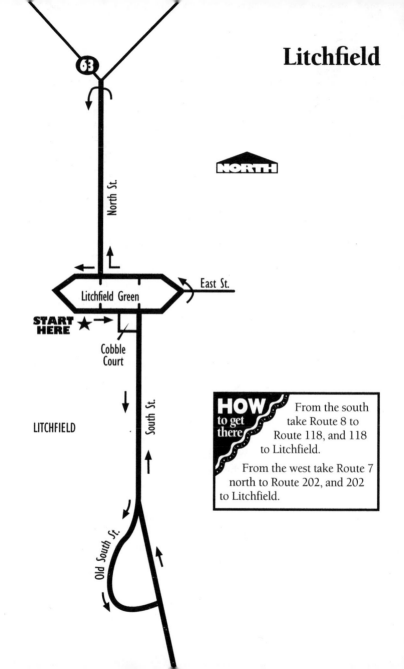

Litchfield

NORTH

North St.

Litchfield Green

East St.

START HERE ★→

Cobble Court

South St.

LITCHFIELD

Old South St.

HOW to get there — From the south take Route 8 to Route 118, and 118 to Litchfield.

From the west take Route 7 north to Route 202, and 202 to Litchfield.

brother-in-law, Aaron Burr, was his first pupil. It matriculated more than one thousand students before it closed in 1833.

When you get to the intersection of South Street and Old South Street, notice the Ethan Allen House, built in 1736. This house is believed to have been the birthplace of the Revolutionary War hero. Bear right and follow Old South Street for approximately 1³/₁₀ miles as it loops back to South Street, where you turn left and go uphill back to the green. On South Street the sidewalk is broad and passes close to the lovely old houses; it's a good place to ride if there is not too much pedestrian traffic. Watch for the Oliver Wolcott, Sr., House (Wolcott, governor of Connecticut, was a signer of the Declaration of Independence). Turn right when you arrive at the green, circle around the end of the green and proceed to the intersection with North Street (Route 63 north). There are stately homes on both sides of North Street, including, on the west side, Sheldon's Tavern where George Washington once slept. Go up one side of North Street and down the other, using the Alexander Catlin House (1778) at the Y as the turn-around point. Return to the green.

Litchfield County

Number of miles:	12
Approximate pedaling time:	2 hours
Terrain:	definitely hilly
Surface:	mostly good, some bad spots
Things to see:	superb Connecticut farmland and woods, fine houses of Litchfield

If you would like a leisurely, French-countryside kind of a picnic, under a tall shady tree with cows lowing on the other side of a New England stone wall, load your pannier bags with all the fixings and take this ride, starting from the Litchfield Green. But first a word about parking your motorized vehicle: The town of Litchfield has instituted one- and two-hour limits for parking around the small green, so I suggest that you park behind one of the nearby churches.

Turn left onto Route 202 and ride approximately 1 mile to the point where Brush Hill Road angles off at forty-five degrees to your right. Turn right onto Brush Hill Road, and in about ½ mile you will pass a long, low stone wall on the left. This was once the site of the Kilravock Inn. In the original edition of our book the Litchfield rides started from this inn. Alas, the beautiful inn burned to the ground several years ago and is no more.

After 1½ miles of uphill riding through the woods, Brush Hill becomes Maple Street at a stop sign. Continue on Maple Street, passing Litwin Road on the left. Soon you will come to the intersection of Maple and Milton Road. Turn right onto Milton, which meanders, going uphill and down (as do all these roads). You will pass the Stony Brook Golf Course. Two miles after turning onto Milton, you will

Litchfield County

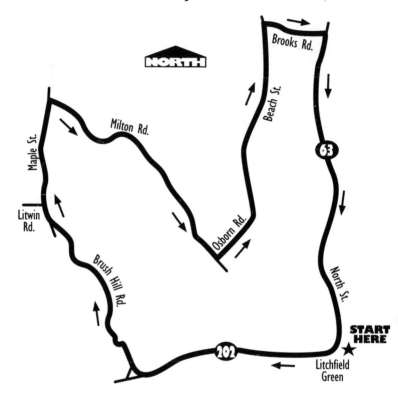

NORTH

Brooks Rd.

Beach St.

Milton Rd.

Maple St.

63

Litwin
Rd.

Osborn Rd.

Brush Hill Rd.

North St.

**START
HERE**

202

Litchfield
Green

HOW
to get
there

From the south take Route 8
to Route 118, and 118 to
Litchfield.

From the west take Route 7 north to
Route 202, and 202 to Litchfield.

come to Osborn Road on your left. Turn up Osborn for a short, steep push. Within ½ mile Osborn merges with Beach Street.

As you join Beach Street, you will bear slightly left, and in approximately 1 mile you'll come to the lovely spot where your authors picnicked when creating the ride. Our lunch under a stately tree was accompanied by the lowing of a clutch of mildly curious cows on the other side of the stone wall.

Back on the road, you'll enjoy the views occasionally revealed through the trees and the large country homes you will pass. Two miles from the intersection of Osborn and Beach, you come to Brooks Road; turn right. The street sign here may be twisted, showing the street names reversed, but 'tis not so. You *have* been on Beach Street and *are* turning onto Brooks Road, which immediately goes downhill and then abruptly uphill before descending again to Route 63. Brooks Road forms a T with Route 63. Turn right. There is a stop sign for you; be cautious.

You are about 3 miles from Litchfield, and you face a couple of arduous uphill climbs, barely relieved by brief downhills. In Litchfield, Route 63, also called Goshen Road, becomes North Street. This street is flanked by some of America's architectural treasures. From the size and immaculate condition of all these eighteenth- and nineteenth-century homes, it appears that only the houses of the wealthy were worth preserving over such a long period of time, creating a Litchfield of today very different from what it was 200 years ago.

Salisbury–Falls Village

Number of miles: 19
Approximate pedaling time: 2½ hours
Terrain: varied, some tough hills, some rolling country, some flat stretches
Surface: generally good
Things to see: Salisbury and Falls Village, Great Falls, Lime Rock Park, Berkshire foothills, Salmon Creek Valley

This is mountain country, Connecticut style. It isn't the Rockies or the Alps, but it's beautiful—as you will soon see. Park anywhere on Main Street and head northeast on Route 44. In a half mile you'll go uphill and crest at the entrance to Salisbury School. Parts of the climb are very steep but are followed by a mile-long downhill with a view of the Berkshires. Half a mile from the bottom you'll cross the Housatonic River and make a right turn onto Route 126 heading for Falls Village. In 1½ miles you'll cross a single railroad track and come to the junction with Sand Road, which comes in from the left. Bear right and cross the bridge over the Hollenbeck River. Off the road, on the left, is a small white sign: STATE OWNED PROPERTY—HUNTING PERMITTED. So, this stretch of river belongs to you and me and it's a lovely spot for a picnic—and, if you're so inclined, a dip in an old-fashioned swimming hole. Your authors did both one Fourth of July, and nary a car went by.

Continue on 126 and when it turns left, go straight on Point of Rocks Road downhill to a **Y** fork. Bear right, under the railroad, ninety degrees right, past the hydroelectric power plant and left across the one-lane bridge. The tiny riverside park on the left has rest

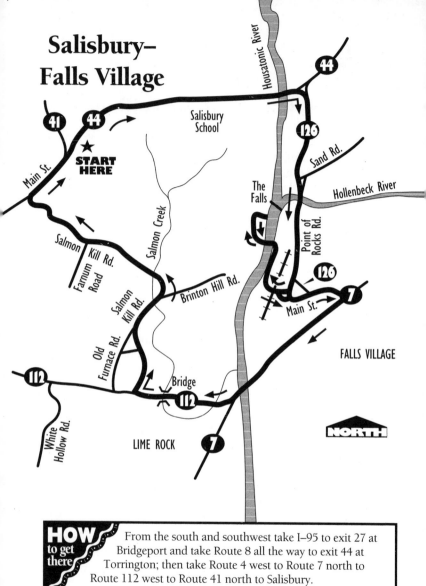

Salisbury–Falls Village

41 · 44

★ START HERE

Main St.

Salisbury School

Housatonic River

44

126

Sand Rd.

Hollenbeck River

The Falls

Point of Rocks Rd.

Salmon Creek

Salmon Kill Rd.

Farnum Road

Salmon Kill Rd.

Brinton Hill Rd.

126

7

Main St.

FALLS VILLAGE

Old Furnace Rd.

112

Bridge

112

7

NORTH

White Hollow Rd.

LIME ROCK

HOW to get there

From the south and southwest take I–95 to exit 27 at Bridgeport and take Route 8 all the way to exit 44 at Torrington; then take Route 4 west to Route 7 north to Route 112 west to Route 41 north to Salisbury.

From the New Haven area take I–91 north to exit 17, I–691 west to I–84 west to Route 8 at Waterbury, then 8 north.

rooms and an ominous sign, WHEN HORN SOUNDS WATER WILL BE RISING! It's a lovely spot to rest and picnic—just be ready to move if the horn sounds! It means the power plant has stopped diverting the water up at the small dam, and the river will be going over the falls again. To see the falls, go back toward the bridge but don't go over it; turn left and then right. In less than ½ mile you'll see the dam and either a first-class waterfall or a trickle, depending on whether the power plant is operating or not.

In May 1997, I saw the falls of Falls Village for the first time in twenty years: water tumbled and foamed, cascading down the rocks and under the bridge, rushing past the power plant, on its way to the sea.

Retrace your route over the bridge, back under the railroad, and up and right at the Y fork to Main Street, where you turn right. You are now in tiny Falls Village, and across from the National Iron Bank—there is a weathered old shingle church, which is now a rare book shop, R & D Emerson Books. Robert and Dorothy Emerson have been in the book trade more than forty years. Go on in. You are sure to come out with at least one book.

When Main Street rejoins Route 126, take 126 to Route 7. Turn right on Route 7 for Lime Rock 3 miles away. When you come to the junction with Route 112, go right on 112 to Lime Rock.

You'll cross Salmon Creek and ride uphill past the infield entrance to the raceway on your left and a large stone church on your right. As you go downhill across a larger bridge, watch for a narrow, unmarked road on the right immediately after the bridge and before the road that goes sharply downhill on the left to the raceway outfield. Turn right into this unmarked, one-lane road, climbing it steeply uphill to a stop sign and a tiny island like an inverted pyramid with a street sign OLD FURNACE ROAD on the left, SALMON KILL ROAD on the right. Go right on Salmon Kill Road. Soon Brinton Hill Road will go off to the right and you turn sharply left, still on Salmon Kill, crossing the valley floor. For the next 1½ miles you'll wind through lovely country on the west side of the valley before you come to a T at Salisbury's Main Street. Turn right. At the corner of Washinee Street take a drink of the delicious spring water at the public fountain. Continue up Main Street to your starting place.

West Cornwall–
Furnace Creek

Number of miles:	12
Approximate pedaling time:	1½ hours
Terrain:	rolling on the west side of the Housatonic, hilly on the east
Surface:	good
Things to see:	a 160-year-old covered bridge, the Housatonic River, Housatonic Meadows State Park, Furnace Creek, the village of West Cornwall

West Cornwall serves as the starting-off point for two beautiful rides, this one and West Cornwall–Lime Rock. Both come and go through one of the last of the original covered bridges in Connecticut. This one was designed by Ithiel Town and has been in continuous use since 1837.

Park anywhere on West Cornwall's hilly main street. The best place is probably the post office lot, only ⅛ mile from the river. You should explore this tiny village, perched on the side of the restless, beautiful Housatonic River, either before or after your ride. There are interesting shops, including the Tollhouse. The Fresh Fields Restaurant and Gift Shop serves good food—indoors and out. In clear weather you can dine on the restaurant's deck, which is built out over a rocky brook and waterfall. A stop here is a great reward, especially after your ride. Another plus on this ride is that there are numerous lovely places to picnic, either on the banks of the Housatonic or along Furnace Creek.

Start the ride by crossing the river over the covered bridge. Turn left on the other side and go south on Route 7 along the river's edge.

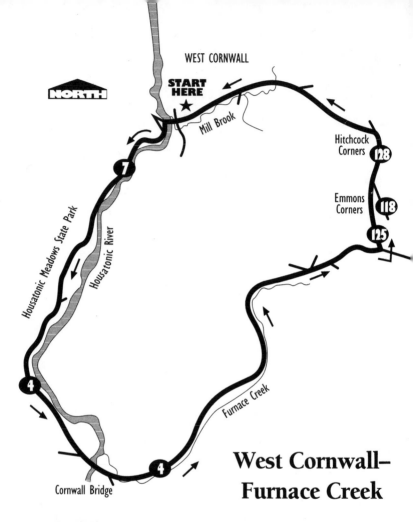

WEST CORNWALL

NORTH

START HERE ★

Mill Brook

7

Housatonic Meadows State Park

Housatonic River

Hitchcock Corners **128**

Emmons Corners **118**

125

4

Furnace Creek

4

Cornwall Bridge

West Cornwall–Furnace Creek

HOW to get there
From the north or south take I–91 to the I–691 exit at Meriden. Take I–691 west to I–84 west to Route 8 north to Torrington. Then take Route 4 west to the junction of Routes 4, 43, and 128. Take 128 north to West Cornwall.

From the southeast take Route 8 north from Bridgeport.

You may see canoeists or swimmers tubing where the river is swift but not overly dangerous. You will see very few houses on the ride as the road dips and winds gently uphill and downhill, following the contour of the Housatonic, accompanying it on its long journey to Long Island Sound. It's a magical sight.

In 2½ miles you will come to a campsite that is one of the most inviting we've seen: Housatonic Meadows Campground. One mile further brings you to the park's adjoining picnic grounds for noncampers. In about 4 miles you will come to the junction where Route 4 joins Route 7. Bear left and cross the river at the Cornwall Bridge. Stop on the bridge for a while to take in the scene: river, rocks, clouds above, shades of green, houses tucked into hills.

There is a fork just over the river. Bear left on Route 4 where you must master a steep hill. Route 4 borders Furnace Creek, and there are many superb picnic sites just off the road. We stopped and had lunch about ½ mile from the fork at a lovely spot with a creek right under our feet, just *before* a turnout on the right (with a picnic table in it).

About 8 miles into the ride, you will come to the junction of Routes 4 and 125; turn left and go up a steep hill toward West Cornwall through woods and forest. Soon Route 128 joins 125 at an oblique angle from the right. About ½ mile from town you will start a long winding descent into the village—a great way to end the ride!

West Cornwall–Lime Rock

Number of miles:	16
Approximate pedaling time:	2 hours
Terrain:	definitely hilly, with a long incline and some good downhills
Surface:	good
Things to see:	the hillside village of West Cornwall, the covered bridge, Lime Rock Raceway, the wildlife sanctuary, the splendor of northwest Connecticut's mountains and forests

This ride was suggested by Alan Momeyer and Janet Markoff of New York, who discovered it in the summer of 1983 while using this book as their "main guide for a wonderful four-day weekend of biking."

After arriving in West Cornwall, park your vehicle anywhere along the village's inclined main street—the best place is probably the post office lot, only ⅕ mile from the river. You've got 16 miles of delightful, soul-satisfying bicycle riding to look forward to, so I recommend exploring the little village when you get back.

Start by crossing over the river on the old, one-lane covered bridge, turning right on the other side to go north on Route 7. The Housatonic is within earshot on your right, and silent forests tower up on your left. For 4 miles your road rolls up and down, changing every ⅕ mile! At the 4-mile point, you'll come to the junction of Route 112 with 7 north, which curves right. You should bear left onto 112.

For 2 miles this road will prove wider, flatter, and smoother than the forest roller coaster you've just left, but it provides a pleasant change with its lovely picture-postcard homes from the late nine-

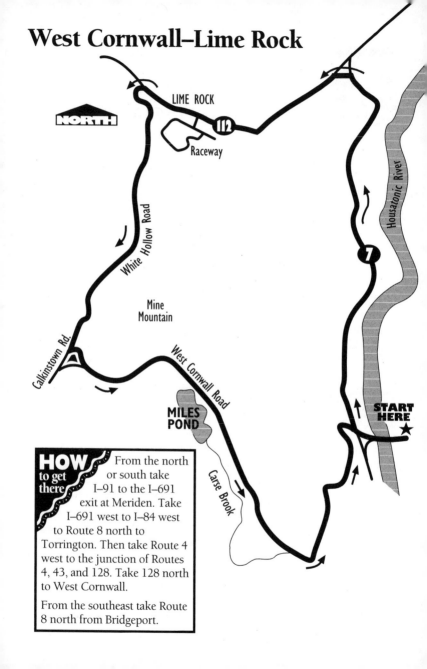

West Cornwall–Lime Rock

NORTH

LIME ROCK

112

Raceway

White Hollow Road

Housatonic River

7

Mine
Mountain

Calkinstown Rd.

West Cornwall Road

**MILES
POND**

Carse Brook

**START
HERE** ★

HOW to get there — From the north
or south take
I–91 to the I–691
exit at Meriden. Take
I–691 west to I–84 west
to Route 8 north to
Torrington. Then take Route 4
west to the junction of Routes
4, 43, and 128. Take 128 north
to West Cornwall.

From the southeast take Route
8 north from Bridgeport.

teenth century. Within $1\frac{1}{4}$ miles at the crest of a hill, Lime Rock Raceway comes into view over on the left. As Alan and Janet put it, the raceway "might be a fun pit stop." About $\frac{3}{4}$ mile farther on, 2 miles from Route 7, you'll cross over a bridge and immediately make a hairpin left turn downhill onto White Hollow Road, which then quickly twists to the right, still going downhill. For the next $4\frac{1}{2}$ miles you'll be on a roller coaster once again, passing beautiful early twentieth-century homes surrounded by tall trees with sculpted farmland in the background. Then you'll come to a T intersection with a little grassy island separating two country roads, West Cornwall Road, which you will take to the left, and Calkinstown Road to the right (White Hollow Road, having done its work, ends here).

Once you have turned left onto West Cornwall Road, get ready! You're about to enter a primeval swamp and forest preserve, 5 miles of wildlife sanctuary with "all plants and animals protected by state and federal law and by the National Audubon Society." The preserve lies within a valley between the mountains of the Housatonic State Forest. Mine Mountain is the one you can see rising up behind the first swamp on the left. You will probably be the only human being on the road. Bring binoculars, ride slowly, and absorb the mysteries of the wildlife.

In about $1\frac{1}{2}$ miles, Miles Pond will appear on the right, then Carse Brook, and then suddenly a startling sight appears—a magnificent, two-story stone house bearing an air of antiquity about it, quiet, out of place, as though materialized by Prospero's magic from seventeenth-century England. It's just off the road; next to it is a stone swimming pool, guarded by two large bronze statues, and then you'll see a sign: MILES WILDLIFE SANCTUARY.

About 1 mile after you enter the land of private property once again, the road heads sharply downhill to the left, zigzags steeply down ninety degrees to the left, cuts a hard right, levels off, and then goes steeply down and to the right again, ending abruptly at a T with Route 7. You'll find yourself just across from the covered bridge to West Cornwall!

Avon–Simsbury

Number of miles:	20
Approximate pedaling time:	2 hours
Terrain:	mostly gentle, one notably long hill
Surface:	fair
Things to see:	Avon, Avon Park, Avon Old Farms School, Simsbury, Massacoh Plantation, Ethel Walker School, Stratton Brook State Park

Avon–Simsbury has much to offer, from the sight of a small seventeenth-century English village that turns out to be a boys' school to 6¼ miles of bike paths, including one that was a secret path known only to those living near it or you, dear reader. Alas, by mid-1998, this path will no longer be a secret one.

The best place to start is from the parking lot at the Old Avon Village Shopping Center, which is located a short distance back from the southeast corner of the intersection of Routes 44 and 202, where 44 goes straight and 202 turns and goes north.

Come out of the parking lot, turn left using the sidewalk (walking your bike), go the short distance to the intersection of 44 and 202, and turn left onto Old Farms Road. In less than a ½ mile you'll come to Arch Street on the right. A 1¾ mile section of the Farmington Valley Greenway begins here. Ride over to it and turn left for a traffic-free ride to Avon Old Farms School, which is marked by an enormous brick tower. Pass the tower and turn left into the driveway and ride up to the main building. This boys' school is built in the style of an Elizabethan village. It is an enchanting sight. Leave by the exit driveway, turn right at the gate, and ride the few yards to Scoville Road. Turn left onto Scoville; in ½ mile, turn right onto Burnham

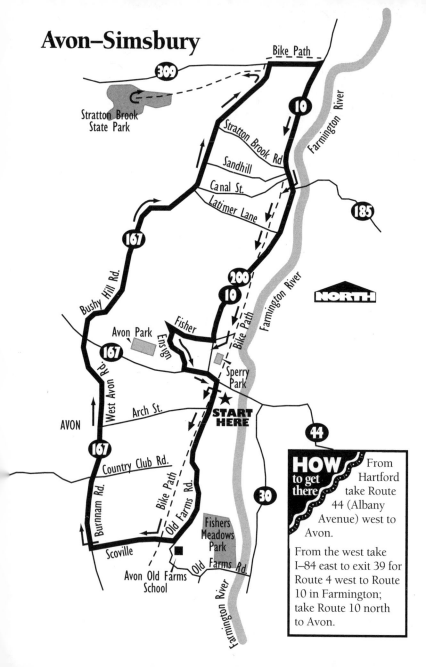

Avon–Simsbury

Bike Path

309

Stratton Brook State Park

Farmington River

10

Stratton Brook Rd

Sandhill

Canal St.

Latimer Lane

185

167

Bushy Hill Rd.

200

10

Farmington River

NORTH

Fisher

Avon Park

Ensign

West Avon Rd.

167

Sperry Park

Arch St.

★ START HERE

AVON

44

167

Country Club Rd.

Bike Path

Burnham Rd.

Old Farms Rd.

30

Fishers Meadows Park

Scoville

Avon Old Farms School

Old Farms Rd.

Farmington River

HOW to get there

From Hartford take Route 44 (Albany Avenue) west to Avon.

From the west take I–84 east to exit 39 for Route 4 west to Route 10 in Farmington; take Route 10 north to Avon.

Road. When Burnham forms a T with West Avon Road (Route 167), turn right.

Cross Route 44 and head toward Simsbury on Route 167 (now called Bushy Hill Road). There is a long incline on this stretch. You'll pass the Ethel Walker School, cross Stratton Brook Road, and, in about a mile, come to the T intersection with Route 309. Within a few feet of this intersection, on the left side of Route 167, there is a small opening in the trees. This is the beginning of a hidden bike path, running for a mile straight to Stratton Brook State Park. Cross the road and get on the bike path from Bickford Road. The transition is swift and startling—from asphalt, traffic, and noise to the hush of a leafy wonderland. The trail of hard-packed earth ends at the lake in the center of the park. Here you may swim, hike, and picnic. The rest rooms and dressing cubicles across the pond are closed after Labor Day, the park department has supplied two outhouses for those who like to ride in the fall or winter.

Return to Route 167 on the bike trail. As soon as you're back on 167, turn right at the T with 309, riding on the paved bike path that runs alongside 309, to the junction of 309 and 202/10. At the stoplight marking the intersection of Routes 309 and 202, you have a choice: turn right and head toward Avon, 4 miles away, or take a left and detour through the town of Simsbury and visit the Massacoh Plantation, an interesting museum on Simsbury's Main Street. After returning to the intersection of Routes 309 and 202, proceed south on 202. If the traffic is heavy you can ride on the sidewalk for the first 1¾ miles, after which you'll be at Canal Street and the start of a 2¼-mile paved bike path off to the right of 202/10 which takes you all the way to Avon Park. Just before Sperry Park on the right, there is a turn off to Fisher Drive which you take and then turn left onto Ensign Drive. You'll soon see the renovated factory complex now harboring Avon Park and the Farmington Arts Center. The town offices are also here—complete with rest rooms. There are exhibits in the gallery of the Arts Center and artists' studios in the adjoining brownstones. (This delightful complex used to be a fuse factory!) Go out the park's exit to Route 44, turn left, and return to the Old Avon Village Shopping Center 1½ blocks away.

Farmington

Number of miles:	13½
Approximate pedaling time:	2 hours
Terrain:	varied, some short steep hills
Surface:	good
Things to see:	Batterson Park, Stanley-Whitman House, Miss Porter's School, Hill-Stead Museum, the Grist Mill

Farmington is one of those Connecticut towns and villages that were founded before the American Revolution and bear the label "quaint" but are indeed far more than that tainted word implies. Farmington, like many others, is inhabited by people who care about the part their town played in American history and about maintaining the buildings and traditions from the past, but they also live very much in the present—all of which makes their town a fascinating place to explore.

You'll be starting the ride from the Park-and-Ride parking lot on Fieneman Road, where Batterson Park Road joins Fieneman at exit 37 off I–84. East of here Fieneman Road is called Farmington Avenue—one of the idiosyncrasies of life in Connecticut. Whatever it's called, come out of Park and Ride and turn right on it, crossing over I–84 on the sidewalk if you deem it wise. Within ½ mile you'll come to the intersection of Fieneman, Colt Highway (Route 6), and Birdseye. Cross Colt Highway at a forty-five-degree angle onto Birdseye, then turn left onto Mountain Road, the first left.

After a mile turn left at the stop sign onto Reservoir Road, keeping a sharp eye out for traffic coming up the road from your right. In about a mile turn right onto Route 6, Colt Highway. At the intersection of Routes 6 and 10, turn right onto Route 10. Within a mile

Farmington

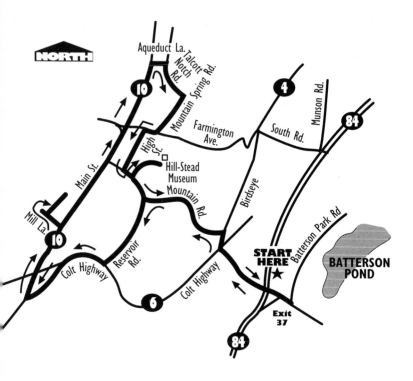

NORTH

Aqueduct La.
Talcott Notch Rd.
Mountain Spring Rd.
10
4
Munson Rd.
84
Farmington Ave.
South Rd.
High St.
Hill-Stead Museum
Mountain Rd.
Main St.
Birdseye
Mill La.
10
Reservoir Rd.
Colt Highway
Colt Highway
START HERE ★
Batterson Park Rd
BATTERSON POND
6
Exit 37
84

HOW to get there From the north take Route 84 to exit 37 (Fieneman Road) and cross Fieneman Road to the Park-and-Ride lot, corner of Batterson Park Road and Fieneman Road.

From the south take I–91 to the Meriden exit for I–691 west. Take 691 west to I–84 and 84 north to exit 37.

Route 10 becomes Main Street, and you'll be in the beautiful town of Farmington. Take a side trip to the Grist Mill by turning left on Mill Lane (across from the Congregational church) and going down to the Farmington River. In the mill there's a bookstore, which has carried this book for many years, and a lovely restaurant. Back on Main Street (Route 10), ride by the Congregational church and the buildings of Miss Porter's School.

Cross Route 4 (Farmington Avenue) at the traffic light and continue on Route 10 north about 2 miles, past the golf course, to Aqueduct Lane. Turn right, and go up this short but steep hill to a T intersection with Talcott Notch Road, where you turn right. At Mountain Spring Road, turn right again, and within another 1½ miles you'll be back at Farmington Avenue. Turn right onto Farmington, go down a short, steep hill to High Street, where you turn left at the caution light, exercising extreme caution.

Midway up High Street you'll see the Stanley-Whitman House (1660). Open to the public on Sunday only, there is a small fee.

When you reach Mountain Road (a T intersection), turn left and go a short distance uphill to the entrance driveway to the Hill-Stead Museum. Turn left and ride through the grounds to the Stanford White–designed house. Hill-Stead is an unusual museum in that the owners stipulated that it was to remain exactly as it had been when they lived in it, with their beautiful paintings and sculpture by Manet, Monet, Degas, and other French Impressionists in their original settings. It is open May through October, noon to 5:00 P.M. and November through April, noon to 4:00 P.M. A moderate admission fee is charged.

When you are ready, continue the ride by going back along the entrance driveway to Mountain Road, where you turn left. Mountain Road lives up to its name now, illustrating the old saw that "what goes up must come down"—the up side of the mountain. It is actually a hill, but it is steep. This is the same Mountain Road that you came in on, and it will take you back to Birdseye where you turn right then across Colt Highway and left on Fieneman Road and the Park and Ride.

Pleasant Valley

Number of miles:	10
Approximate pedaling time:	1½ hours
Terrain:	rolling, not very steep
Surface:	good
Things to see:	beautiful Farmington River, Peoples State Forest and American Legion State Forest, Hitchcock Chair Factory, and the small towns of Riverton and Pleasant Valley

This ride, which was suggested to me by Christopher Devine of Kensington, will live up to its name. It is a very pleasant, soul-enriching voyage through Pleasant Valley, which has a crystal-clear river flowing through its center, dividing the forest into two very different halves, so much so that one side is called the American Legion State Forest and the other the Peoples State Forest.

Once you are driving on Route 318, it's a short distance to the tiny town of Pleasant Valley. As you come downhill you'll see the Barkhamstead town hall and school on your right, then the General Store/Pleasant Valley Post Office on the right-hand corner of 318 and West River Road. Turn right on West River Road and drive the short distance to the United Methodist Church and cemetery. Park in its lot.

Ride back up West River Road past the bridge on the right. You'll be skirting the meandering river for a while through the American Legion Forest under a canopy of tall trees that form themselves into a green Gothic cathedral. As the route moves back and forth—close to the riverbank then away—small islands appear and disappear.

After about 4½ miles you come to a T with Highway 20. Turn

Pleasant Valley

Riverton Rd.

Hitchcock ■
Factory

20

West River Rd.

East River Rd.

NORTH

West River Rd.

East River Rd.

West River Rd.

East River Rd.

West River Rd.

East River Rd.

Whittmore
Recreation
Area

GeneralStore/
Post Office
318

44

**START
HERE** ★ ✝

44

HOW
to get
there
From the south take I–95 or Route 15 to Route 8 north, to Route 44 or Winsted. Take Route 44 east (3 miles) to Route 318, on left, to Pleasant Valley. From the northeast take I-95 to I-691 west at Meriden. Take I-691 west to I-84 to Route 8 north to Route 44.

right. On your left is the man-made attraction of this delightful ride, the Hitchcock Chair Factory. They make a variety of furniture and have been doing so on this site for a very long time. Do go in and visit. If you have time, visit the rest of Riverton before continuing down the east side of the river.

When you're ready to continue, ride across the bridge and turn right onto East River Road. Now you are riding through the Peoples Forest. The road is narrower than the one on the west side, but it is lightly traveled and mostly downhill, with tall fir trees on both side— trees that bend slightly toward each other at their high high tops as though they are getting ready for a madrigal, or perhaps whispering tree things to each other.

This upper section of West Brook is well known to fishermen, many of whom stand up to their waists in the cold water kept dry by their chest-high waders. When I first rode this ride, I stopped at a riverbank picnic table for a bit of lunch. There was but one table, and it faced an opening in the trees about as wide as a small stage with trees for the proscenium arch. As I sat there, eating my sandwich, three people in a canoe came on the scene from the right, paddled across my stage, and rapidly disappeared only to be followed by a second canoe, which appeared to be full of Shakespearean actors in hot pursuit!

My next stop was farther downstream at the Whittmore Recreation Area, which offered six or seven picnic tables, several stone fireplaces, a nice riverfront beach, and two rustic outhouses.

After my stop here I soon came to the T with Pleasant Valley Road (Route 318), turned right, crossed over the river on the bridge, then left on West River Road the short distance to my starting place.

Wethersfield

Number of miles: 11½
Approximate pedaling time: 1½ hours
Terrain: varied, some steep hills
Surface: generally good, some poor spots
Things to see: Buttolph-Williams House, Silas Deane House, Joseph Webb House, Isaac Stevens House, Old Academy Museum, Comstock-Ferre Co., Wethersfield Cove, Millwoods Park

Wethersfield is one of the towns where history was made, and there's much to see. Start the ride on Main Street across from the Comstock-Ferre Co., Connecticut's oldest seed company and a good place to browse. Ride north on Main Street past many handsome houses to the shore of Wethersfield Cove and Common. This is a busy boating scene in the summer. Return down Main Street and turn left on Marsh Street. Ride past the cemetery and turn right on Broad Street. The marvelous Buttolph-Williams House (1710) stands silently on the corner. This house contains an excellent collection of period pieces, including an extensively furnished kitchen. Proceed on Broad Street to the Wethersfield Green. Bear left and ride down the left side of the green. At the end turn right and come back up the right side as far as Garden Street. Turn left on Garden and go to Main. Turn right. Pass the Old Academy Museum. In another block you will come to a trio of stately houses. The Silas Deane House (1766) is the first of these. General Benedict Arnold, assisted by his good friend Silas Deane, planned the capture of Fort Ticonderoga in this elegant house. The Joseph Webb House (1752) was also graced by the presence of

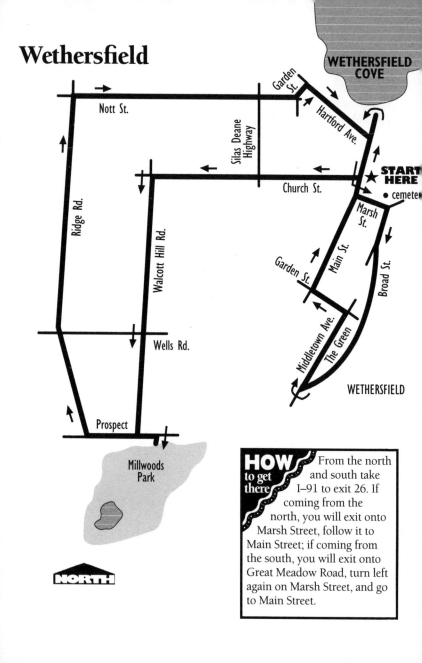

Wethersfield

WETHERSFIELD COVE

Garden St.

Nott St.

Hartford Ave.

Silas Deane Highway

Ridge Rd.

START HERE

• cemetery

Church St.

Marsh St.

Walcott Hill Rd.

Main St.

Garden St.

Broad St.

Middletown Ave.

The Green

WETHERSFIELD

Wells Rd.

Prospect

Millwoods Park

NORTH

HOW to get there From the north and south take I–91 to exit 26. If coming from the north, you will exit onto Marsh Street, follow it to Main Street; if coming from the south, you will exit onto Great Meadow Road, turn left again on Marsh Street, and go to Main Street.

General Washington, for here he met with Rochambeau in 1781 to plan the last campaigns of the Revolution. The Isaac Stevens House (1788), while more modest, has an interesting collection of children's clothes and paraphernalia. Don't neglect to take note of the nineteenth-century elegance of the Hurlbut–Dunham House across the street from the Stevens House.

Now proceed to the intersection with Church Street and turn left. Go uphill. Cross the Silas Deane Highway. Go uphill again to Walcott Hill Road; turn left. At the crest of the hill, cross Wells Road and go downhill to Prospect Street, where there is a traffic light. Turn left at Prospect and then right into Millwoods Park. Here you may picnic but no longer swim. Alas, the town has changed to a "residents only" policy. In the picnic area on the other side of the pond there are some rest rooms (open in the summer months only).

After visiting Millwoods Park, turn left onto Prospect Street, ride uphill to Ridge Road and turn right. The road crests at Wells Street. You will start downhill after crossing Rutledge. Turn right on Nott Street, where, after a brief uphill spurt, you get a nice downhill run. Cross the Silas Deane Highway again, go to Garden Street, the last street on your left before Hartford Avenue, and turn left. Garden Street may not be marked. Cross Hartford Avenue and go in the entrance driveway to the Solomon Wells House (1774), which is now used only for local functions. The expanse of lawn down to the cove is a good picnic spot, however. When you're ready to leave, turn left on Hartford Avenue, which will lead you to Main Street and your car.

Hopeville Pond–Jewett City

Number of miles: 11
Approximate pedaling time: 1½ hours
Terrain: half downhill and half uphill
Surface: good
Things to see: Hopeville Pond State Park, Jewett City, dairy farms, forests

I discovered Hopeville Pond by a serendipitous wrong turn during a fruitless attempt to create a new ride. Finding myself on the wrong road, I looked for the first place to turn around and came upon the entrance to the park. I decided to explore it and found what I had been searching for—the beginning and ending place for a new ride!

Just inside the entrance on the left, there's a large playing field with a good-sized parking lot. To begin the ride, however, drive further into the park where you will find large restrooms, and well-laid-out, swimming, sunbathing, picnicking, and camping areas all bordering the lake—which you can explore by renting a canoe. I had a picnic lunch at a table that rested on a carpet of pine needles. The photograph to the left of this page gives you the picture. You can park in the lot that overlooks the lake and when you're all set to go, ride back to the entrance. If you look to your left, you'll see low stone walls, fashioned by hand about 120 years ago. They meander silently through most of the woodlands of Connecticut, all that's left of the farms that were abandoned in the 1870s by farmers who were wiped out by the great Depression of that time.

At the entrance turn left onto Route 201, a two-lane road that is not heavily traveled and, happily, goes down hill. The trees that border the road shade you as you ride; Hopeville Pond is visible through the trees.

Hopeville Pond–
Jewett City

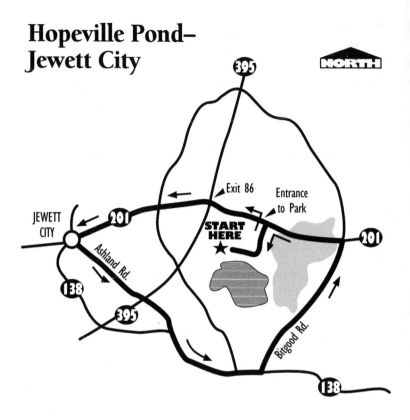

HOW to get there From east or west take I–95 to exit 76, I–395 to exit 86 (Route 201). Go east on 201, 1½ miles to Hopeville Pond State Park.

From north or south take I–395 to exit 86.

In about a mile, you'll see the entrance to Pachaug State Forest on the left. Pachaug has its own lake and all the amenities of Hopeville.

About 2 miles after you leave Hopeville, Route 201 goes under I-395 and begins to curve left as it goes through cow country for another 2 miles to Jewett City. Before you get there, about 1½ miles out from Jewett City, you'll start a steep downhill descent, which levels off at the outskirts of the town. Watch for Ashland Street on your left, where you turn for the beginning of the ride back to Hopeville. If you find yourself at the junction with Route 138, with a Sunoco station on the left, you've overshot the mark, so turn around and go right at the next light, which is Ashland. True to Connecticut custom, Ashland will become Taylor Hill Road as it goes over I-395, downhill, then uphill to Route 138, where you turn left and ride along its wide shoulder for about 3½ miles to Bitgood Road—watch for it on the left just after you go over a little bridge. Bitgood will take you downhill as it curves around Hopeville Pond for about 1½ miles to Route 201, where you turn left and back to your starting place for a swim or what-have-you.

Pomfret–Woodstock

Number of miles: 15
Approximate pedaling time: 2 hours
Terrain: varied, some of it quite demanding
Surface: good
Things to see: Pomfret School, Woodstock, Bowen Mansion, Roseland Park and Lake, Wappaquasset Pond

There are places in Pomfret and Woodstock where time seems to have passed very slowly. Come see. Start the ride at the Pomfret post office, which is located on Route 44 just east of the junctions of Routes 44 and 169. Return to the junction, then turn right onto 169 north, which is a real roller coaster of a hill as you leave town. At about the 3-mile mark, you will come to a stop sign, where Route 171 crosses 169. Turn left and continue on 169 to the town of Woodstock. You will see a pink Victorian mansion on the left. This is the Bowen Mansion, built by Henry Bowen in 1846. There are extensive herb and flower gardens on the grounds, and at various time during the year you may be guided through the mansion by actors in period clothing. It is open to the public from mid-May to mid-September, Wednesday through Sunday, noon to 5:00 P.M., and from September to mid-October, Friday through Sunday, noon to 5:00 P.M.

Leaving Woodstock, take a right on Child Hill Road at the end of the Green and ride downhill for a fast, magnificent 1½-mile run. At the bottom of the hill turn right onto Roseland Park Road at the stop sign. In a mile you can enter the park on your left. Roseland Park was endowed by Henry Bowen of the pink mansion in Woodstock, and it has retained its turn-of-the-century ambience. As of 1997, all the

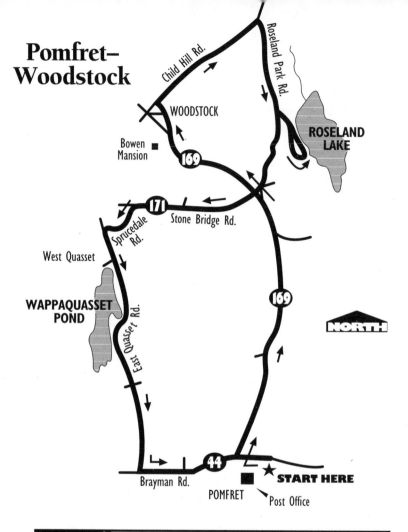

Pomfret–Woodstock

Child Hill Rd.

Roseland Park Rd.

WOODSTOCK

ROSELAND LAKE

Bowen Mansion ■

169

171

Stone Bridge Rd.

Sprucedale Rd.

West Quasset

WAPPAQUASSET POND

East Quasser Rd.

169

NORTH

44

Brayman Rd.

★ **START HERE**

■

POMFRET

Post Office

HOW to get there Pomfret is a few miles west of Putnam. From the south take I–395 to exit 93 (Killingly Center), then take Route 101 west to Route 169, and turn north to Pomfret.

From the west take Route 86 to exit 100, and take Route 44 east to Pomfret.

buildings in the park have been painted pink—to match the pink Bowen Mansion! The park's golf course, built in 1891, is said to be the oldest in the United States. Here you can picnic on the soft, sloping bank of the pond—a lovely, tranquil place. Head back to the road and turn left to resume your ride.

Turn right at Stone Bridge Road at the common in South Woodstock. Cross Route 169. Now you face a real gear-shifter of a hill. Watch for Sprucedale Road on the left. Turn forty-five degrees onto Sprucedale, which soon forms a T with East Quasset Road. Turn left on East Quasset and go up a steep hill, to the left, at the fork with West Quasset, past the cemetery to the top of the ridge. Wappaquasset Pond is on your right. This 2½-mile stretch is a winding country road, with a view of rolling meadows bounded by low stone walls, cows, and huge trees. East Quasset Road comes to a T at Brayman Road; turn left and gear up for a steep climb back to Pomfret. Before you go take a look to your right at what appears to be a castle on a hill.

Brayman is also Route 44 on which you cross Route 169, back to your starting place.

15 Thompson–Quaddick State Park

Number of miles:	12
Approximate pedaling time:	1½ hours
Terrain:	rolling; long downhill at start, uphill near end
Surface:	good
Things to see:	the stately town of Thompson, Quaddick State Park, Thompson International Raceway

The town of Thompson and the adjoining forest and lake of Quaddick are nestled in the far northeastern corner of Connecticut, on the border of Rhode Island and Massachusetts. The ride will take you to where change comes at a measured pace. Near its end, however, close to an old cemetery for those who died in the French and Indian Wars, you will see a place where change comes at a furious pace—the Thompson International Raceway, home to the Nascar Winston 300.

On weekdays, you can begin the ride at the Quaddick State Park. The fee for parking your vehicle is in effect only on weekends ($5.00 for Connecticut plates, $8.00 out of state). Or you can begin the ride from the parking lot behind the 1856 Congregational church on the east side of the Thompson Common, at the corner of Routes 193 and 200. (Taking this ride on a weekday makes it possible to start from the park and picnic there at the end of the ride without paying the fee for parking.) I'd suggest a picnic on the Thompson Green at the end of your ride, or lunch or dinner at the Vernon Stiles Inn, a travelers' rest stop since 1814, if you begin from the Congregational church.

Let's assume that you are starting from the church and will tour the town at the end of the ride. When you're saddled up, leave the

Thompson–Quaddick State Park

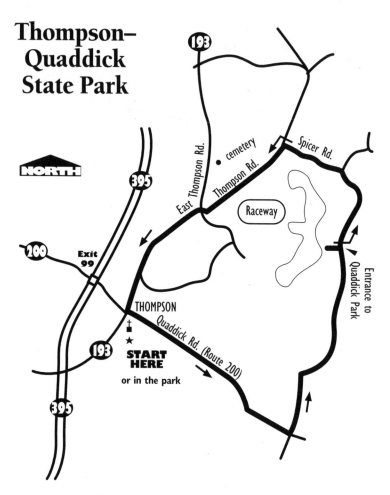

HOW to get there

From north or south take I–395 to exit 99. Go east on Route 200 to Thompson.

From east or west take I–95 to exit 76, I–395 north. Take I–395 to exit 99.

parking lot and turn right onto Route 200, a smooth road that offers you a fast 2½-mile downhill before beginning to roll up and down for another ¾ mile to a stop sign and a sign indicating that Quaddick State Park is to your left. Turn left and ride the 1½ miles to the park entrance. The park is big enough to accommodate a large crowd—as I saw on Memorial Day, the first day the park opens—but most of the people cluster over on the left side near the beach. There are plenty of picnic tables, spread far apart among the trees, available at the water's edge to the right of the entrance. In addition to picnicking and swimming, Quaddick has a snack bar, rest rooms, and canoe rentals.

When ready to continue, turn left at the entrance to the park. After a couple of miles the road goes right then comes to a Y where Spicer Road comes in from the left. Turn onto Spicer Road and take it, uphill, to where it forms a T into Thompson Road. Turn left. At your right is a cemetery—a most unusual cemetery. As the bronze plaque simply states, the cemetery is dedicated

TO THOSE

WHO FOUGHT IN THE

FRENCH AND INDIAN

WARS

THE REVOLUTIONARY WAR

THE WAR OF 1812

THE

WAR OF THE REBELLION

AND THE

SPANISH AMERICAN

WAR

Your road goes steeply uphill now. The forest has gone and in its stead, far over on the left, is the Thompson Raceway, where stock car races are held every Wednesday night from March 27 through October. On one of those nights the Nascar Winston 300 is held, bringing the big-time racers to Thompson. Several miles after you pass the entrance to the raceway, you come in at an angle to a four-way intersection. You make a short jog to the right and then left onto Route 193, East Thompson Road, which will take you back to the common, or green as it is also called, of Thompson.

Storrs–
University of Connecticut

Number of miles:	12
Approximate pedaling time:	1½ hours
Terrain:	definitely hilly
Surface:	good
Things to see:	the University of Connecticut, an old stone mill, tumbling streams, and lovely countryside throughout

The University of Connecticut, unlike Yale, which is older but not necessarily wiser, has its campus out in the countryside where it has *room*. It's a beautiful campus, as is the area around it. As you drive along Route 195 on your way to the starting place at Dog Lane, look for the University Information Centers that are on 195 and stop for a campus map and places to see, such as the William Benton Art Museum.

The best place to start the ride is from Dog Lane, which is just past the main part of the campus, the first light after Mansfield Road and its stop sign at the Publications and Public Relations building. Coming from the direction of I–84, you'd turn left and park behind the stores on Dog Lane.

Mount up and turn left on Dog Lane. Go downhill about ¾ mile to the place where Dog Lane ends at a T intersection; turn right. In about ½ mile you'll come to a stop sign; continue straight ahead. You'll be on Hanks Hill Road, which has come in from the right at the stop sign. You were on Farrell Road (as you must know by now, in Connecticut roads change names or merge into others without warning!).

After another ½ mile you will come to the fork of Hanks Hill Road and Stone Mill Road. Bear right, staying on Hanks Hill. Just past

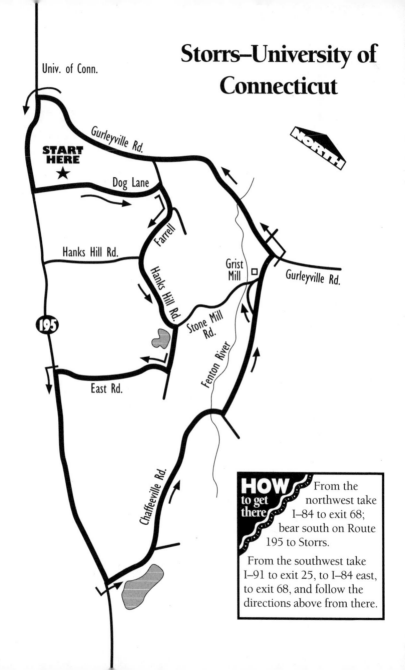

Storrs–University of Connecticut

Univ. of Conn.

Gurleyville Rd.

START HERE ★

Dog Lane

Farrell

Hanks Hill Rd.

Hanks Hill Rd.

Grist Mill

Gurleyville Rd.

195

Stone Mill Rd.

East Rd.

Fenton River

Chaffeeville Rd.

HOW to get there From the northwest take I–84 to exit 68; bear south on Route 195 to Storrs.

From the southwest take I–91 to exit 25, to I–84 east, to exit 68, and follow the directions above from there.

the fork, at the mill pond, there is a sign that states, HERE ON HANKS HILL IN 1810 THE FIRST SILK MILL IN AMERICA WAS BUILT BY RODNEY HANKS. The mill itself is not here because it was removed lock, stone, and board by Henry Ford for his Dearborn Museum.

In another ½ mile, turn right. There's no road sign, but it is East Road. This is a very steep uphill, but there is a grand view at the crest where you can take a rest before turning left onto Route 195 and starting, shortly, a mile-long downhill run. As you tear along, look over to your left and you will see a stunning view of the hills. At the bottom of the hill you continue on the flat for another mile until you come to the intersection of Route 195 and Chaffeeville Road. Turn left onto Chaffeeville, which meanders for 3 miles through the countryside and then curves alongside a little river. Look for a sign, STONE MILL RD.—GRIST MILL, on the left side and a road going steeply down to the river (Stone Mill Road). Take it and you will come upon a serene scene: a narrow stretch of bottomland, a small cheerful river, and an old stone mill. This is the spot for a picnic!

The Gurleyville Grist Mill, built around 1830, is open on Sundays from noon to 4:00 P.M., mid-May to mid-October, and is the state's only remaining stone grist mill.

When you are ready, rejoin Chaffeeville Road and continue on to the next intersection where Chaffeeville, Gurleyville, and Codfish Falls roads meet. Turn left onto Gurleyville. After a short stretch the road starts steeply uphill but soon levels off and then snakes around an enormous meadow as it returns to Route 195 in the middle of the University of Connecticut campus. Here you can make a tour of the campus, or you can turn left onto 195 and ride about ½ mile back to your starting place.

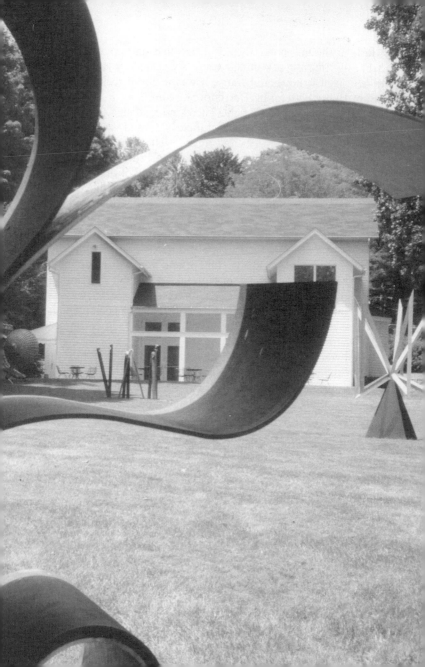

Ridgefield

Number of miles:	12
Approximate pedaling time:	2 hours
Terrain:	definitely hilly
Surface:	good
Things to see:	Ridgefield itself, Aldrich Museum of Contemporary Art, Keeler Tauern Museum, Lake Mamanasco

Ridgefield, like Litchfield and Farmington, is a small, beautifully preserved town full of Revolutionary period history, and parts of it, except for the paved roads and automobiles, look much as they did in 1780.

Start your tour by beginning with the most modern piece of the town, the Aldrich Museum of Contemporary Art, which is on the right side of Main Street, just past the fountain and the point where Route 102 comes into Main. The museum shares the parking lot of the handsome church next door, and you can leave your car there. The contemporary sculpture is displayed in an outdoor garden. When you're ready to ride, turn right onto Main Street and proceed through the shopping area. If the traffic is heavy, use the broad sidewalk, walking your bike. Stop at the Keeler Tavern Museum at 132 Main Street. There's a British cannonball embedded in one of the timbers and there are guided tours in period dress. Turn right at Prospect Street, at the third traffic light. When you come to East Ridge Road, turn right and go uphill. The road soon levels off, then goes downhill to a T intersection with Route 102. Turn right to return to Main Street. Turn left at Main, then right at the fountain where Route 35 joins Main Street. After you pass the Inn at Ridgefield, turn right onto Parley Lane, which angles off at forty-five degrees, then turn immedi-

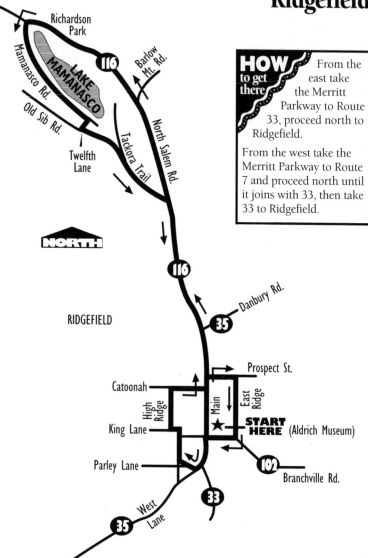

Ridgefield

HOW to get there

From the east take the Merritt Parkway to Route 33, proceed north to Ridgefield.

From the west take the Merritt Parkway to Route 7 and proceed north until it joins with 33, then take 33 to Ridgefield.

Richardson Park

Barlow Mt. Rd.

116

LAKE MAMANASCO

Mamanasco Rd.

Old Sib Rd.

Twelfth Lane

Tackora Trail

North Salem Rd.

NORTH

116

Danbury Rd.

35

RIDGEFIELD

Catoonah

High Ridge

Main

East Ridge

Prospect St.

King Lane

START HERE (Aldrich Museum)

Parley Lane

102

Branchville Rd.

West Lane

33

35

ately right again onto High Ridge Road. Go to the junction of High Ridge and King Lane; continue on High Ridge by snaking left and immediately right. At Catoonah Street turn right and return to Main Street, where you should turn left.

Just past the Elms Inn (which has been in continuous operation since 1799) is the site of the Battle of Ridgefield. In 1777, 600 militiamen under the command of Generals Wooster and Arnold attempted to cut off 1,800 British troops. Wooster was killed, and Arnold and his men finally withdrew as they were outflanked. There is a marker here inscribed: In defense of American independence, at the Battle of Ridgefield, april 27, 1777, died eight patriots who were laid in these grounds companioned by sixteen british soldiers, living their enemies, dying their guests.

The route for the next 4 miles to Lake Mamanasco is mostly downhill (but remember it will be uphill on the way back). When you come to a Y intersection, bear left on Route 116. Watch for the entrance to Richardson Park on the left. This wooded property is open to the public for hiking and picnicking. Turn left onto Mamanasco Road (across from the high school tennis courts). You are about 7 miles into the ride here. This route skirts the beautiful lake.

Turn right at Twelfth Lane at the end of the lake. You'll have to push up this one. At the top of the hill turn left on Old Sib Road, which soon joins Tackora Trail. Bear right on Route 116 at the junction and head back to town. Do stop at the Keeler Tavern (1733) at 133 Main Street. The tavern has been meticulously restored and is open on Wednesdays, weekends, and Monday holidays, from 1:00 to 4:00 P.M. It is truly a must see! Then on to your starting place at the Aldrich Museum.

Rowayton

Number of miles:	8½
Approximate pedaling time:	1 hour
Terrain:	one gradual hill and one very steep climb, otherwise flat
Surface:	fair
Things to see:	Tokeneke (Darien), Wilson Cove, the Sound, village of Rowayton, Five Mile River

Rowayton is one of the many picturesque small towns that wrap themselves around the fingers of land that make up most of Connecticut's long coastline where boats are anchored or moored wherever there's enough water to float them.

We'll start in Darien from the parking lot of the Tokeneke School, which is just off Route 136 (Tokeneke Road). From the parking lot, turn left on Old Farm Road. The area of Tokeneke is dotted with huge houses and equally extravagant NO TRESPASSING signs, but the public roads provide a sufficient glimpse of manorial life. At the T intersection turn left onto Searles Road and right on Five Mile River Road, which reveals a view of the little village of Rowayton on the other side of the river (which is jammed with yachts). Five Mile River Road dead-ends at a turnaround bordered by a stone wall. Turn around and head back up the road. When the road forms a T with Old Farm Road, turn right for a short distance to Tokeneke Road, where you turn right again and cross the bridge into Rowayton. Here the name of the road changes to Cudlipp. At the first light take a sharp left onto Rowayton Avenue. Go gradually uphill several blocks. Turn right on Devil's Garden Road, the fourth road after the railroad

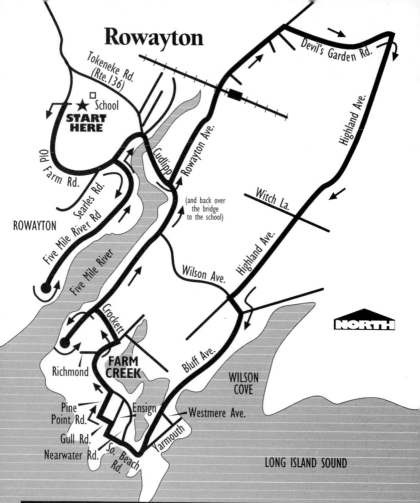

Rowayton

Tokeneke Rd. (Rte.136)

Devil's Garden Rd.

□ School
★ START HERE

Old Farm Rd.

Cudlipp

Rowayton Ave.

Highland Ave.

Seatles Rd.

ROWAYTON

Five Mile River Rd

Five Mile River

(and back over the bridge to the school)

Witch La.

Highland Ave.

Wilson Ave.

NORTH

Crockett

Richmond

FARM CREEK

Bluff Ave.

WILSON COVE

Pine Point Rd.

Ensign

Westmere Ave.

Gull Rd.

Nearwater Rd.

So. Beach Rd.

Yarmouth

LONG ISLAND SOUND

HOW to get there
From the west take I–95 to exit 12, turn right at the foot of the ramp, cross Locust Hill Road, and turn right in about ½ block into the parking lot of the Tokeneke School, where you may park.

From the east take I–95 to exit 11, turn right at the bottom of the ramp, go to Route 136 (before the railroad underpass), and turn right onto 136 (Tokeneke Road); continue on 136 until you come to Old Farm Road on the right; turn right, cross Locust Hill Road, and pull into the parking lot behind the school.

underpass. You'll go steeply uphill now until Devil's Garden forms a T with Highland Avenue; turn right. At the second stop sign, turn left onto Wilson Avenue and go ½ block to Bluff Avenue.

Turn right on Bluff. You'll enjoy the downhill ride back to sea level, where there is a treat in store: you cross over a small bridge at Wilson Cove and from this vantage you can see Bell and Tavern islands and Wilson Point. Bluff changes its name to Westmere when it crosses the bridge; continue straight ahead. As you get close to the water, you come to a stop sign where Yarmouth Road comes in at an angle from the left. Bear right and then right again onto South Beach Road, formerly Crescent Beach Road, named for the shape of this fine little private beach. Continue on as the road goes right as Ensign Road, which is one way against you about half way up, then turn left on Gull Road and right onto Pine Point Road and left at the T with Nearwater. In short order you'll bear right where Richmond comes in from the left, and then after a mercifully short distance you turn left onto Crockett Street, which will lead you to Rowayton Avenue, the village's main thoroughfare.

Turn left so you can explore the eastern end of Rowayton Avenue and the boat yards, then turn around and enjoy the flavor of the village as you pass its appealing yards, yacht brokerages, shops, and restaurants. Stay on Rowayton Avenue until you come to the light marking the intersection with Cudlipp Street; bear left, go over the bridge into Darien, and return to Old Farm Road and the Tokeneke School.

Stratford–Lordship

Number of miles:	12½
Approximate pedaling time:	1½ hours
Terrain:	flat
Surface:	mostly good, some poor paving
Things to see:	Judson House Museum, American Festival Theater, Bridgeport Airport, Long Island Sound at Lordship

There is much to see and do on this ride along the mouth of the Housatonic and the shores of Long Island Sound, so park on West Broad Street if you are here on a weekend or on Academy Hill Road if you should come on a weekday.

Ride the short distance to the T intersection with Main Street; turn right and then left onto Academy Hill Road. On your right halfway up the brief hill stands the Judson House Museum (1723), which is open on Wednesday, Saturday, and Sunday from 11:00 A.M. to 5:00 P.M. There is a small fee.

At the top of Academy Hill turn right onto Elm Street. When you come to the entrance of the American Festival Theater, turn into the grounds. In England this ride might be called Stratford on Housatonic–Lordship on the Sound. In any case, twenty-some years ago, because our Stratford was also on a river and in Connecticut where many theater people reside and so forth, an enlarged version of Shakespeare's Globe Theater was built on the shores of Stratford on Housatonic and called the Stratford Shakespeare Theater. It was—and still is—a marvelous spot for a picnic before the performance, on the lawn under a tall shady tree overlooking the river. The Theater has been closed for many years, but there is good news! It will definitely reopen in the Spring of 1998.

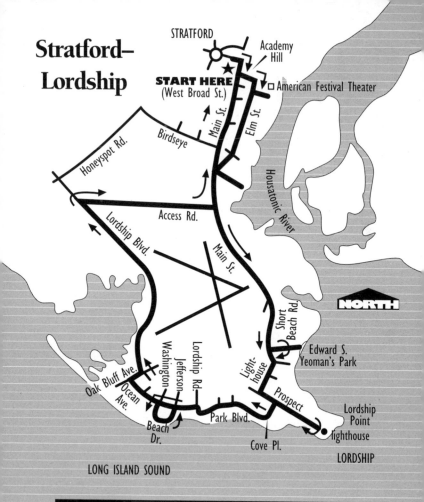

Stratford–Lordship

STRATFORD

START HERE
(West Broad St.)

Academy Hill

American Festival Theater

Main St.

Birdseye

Elm St.

Honeyspot Rd.

Housatonic River

Access Rd.

Lordship Blvd.

Main St.

NORTH

Short Beach Rd.

Edward S. Yeoman's Park

Oak Bluff Ave.

Ocean Ave.

Washington

Jefferson

Lordship Rd.

Light-house

Prospect

Lordship Point lighthouse

Beach Dr.

Park Blvd.

Cove Pl.

LORDSHIP

LONG ISLAND SOUND

HOW to get there
From the east and west take I–95 to exit 32 at Stratford and go to West Broad Street.

From the north take Route 8 to Route 108, go south on 108 to Route 1, cross 1, and bear right on North Parade Street; turn right on Main Street, go under the turnpike, and go to West Broad Street.

On leaving the theater, turn left on Elm Street. In a few blocks, after you pass Tide Harbor condominiums, there is a stop sign; turn left again and ride down to the launching area for a bit of boat watching. Return to Elm Street and turn left. Elm forms a T with Main; turn left. You are now on Stratford Point. After passing the airport you'll come to a Y; ride past it to the next street, Short Beach Road, where you turn left. A short distance down this road is the Stratford town park, the Edward S. Yeoman's Park. Bicyclists are not charged. Turn in and take a look around. There's a beach for swimming, picnic benches under the trees, and a snack bar.

When you come back to the entrance, turn left and ride to Lighthouse Avenue, the last road on the right before the dead end (it may not be marked); turn right. Lighthouse comes to a T at Prospect Drive. Turn left here and proceed to the lighthouse, then turn around and ride back down Prospect to Cove Place on your left. Turn left onto Cove and ride a short stretch to the Sound, where you turn right onto Park Boulevard.

Park Boulevard ends when it forms a T with Lordship Road. Turn right and immediately left on Ocean Avenue. Then turn left again on Washington Parkway. Washington Parkway makes a T with Beach Drive; go left. There is a sea wall here bounded by giant rocks to climb over, fish from, and sit on; and there are a couple of restaurants facing the water. After your R and R at the water's edge, continue on Beach Drive heading east. Turn left on Ocean Avenue and proceed until it forms a T at Oak Bluff Avenue. Turn right. When Oak Bluff intersects with Lordship Boulevard, turn left. You will now cross a great salt marsh. Ride past the airport with the World War II Navy gull wing fighter plane standing guard. If you're ready for a rest stop, there are rest rooms in the terminal.

Continue until you come to the traffic light where Access Road intersects. Turn right, ride to the T with Main Street, and turn left onto Main and ride back to your starting place on either Academy Hill Road or West Broad Street.

Branford

Number of miles:	14
Approximate pedaling time:	2 hours
Terrain:	flat to moderately hilly
Surface:	good
Things to see:	the Blackstone Memorial Library, Branford Green, Bruce and Johnson Marina, Stony Creek, Thimble Islands, Puppet House Theater

Branford is one of the eleven shoreline towns that hug the coast from New Haven to the Rhode Island border, and a lovely old town it is, well worth exploring.

Park near the town hall on the green and ride west on Main Street the short distance to the Blackstone Library on your right. Be sure to go into the auditorium at the rear of the first floor and see this Victorian gem. When you leave the library, turn left toward the green and angle off almost immediately forty-five degrees to the right at the fork onto South Main Street; ride down past the sign SCENIC DRIVE to the T intersection with Montowese Street, and turn right onto what is also Route 146. Follow 146 as it goes under the Amtrak overpass, over the upper end of the Branford River to a big stop sign where Indian Neck Avenue comes in from the right and joins forces with Montowese. Continue around a slight bend to the left about ½ mile till you come to Block Island Road on the right. Turn right *only* if you like to look at boats because the Bruce and Johnson Marina is at the end of the street, and it is full of boats, sail and motor, large and small. Once back to Montowese Road, continue down to a Y where you bear left and then ninety degrees left at the water for a short ride

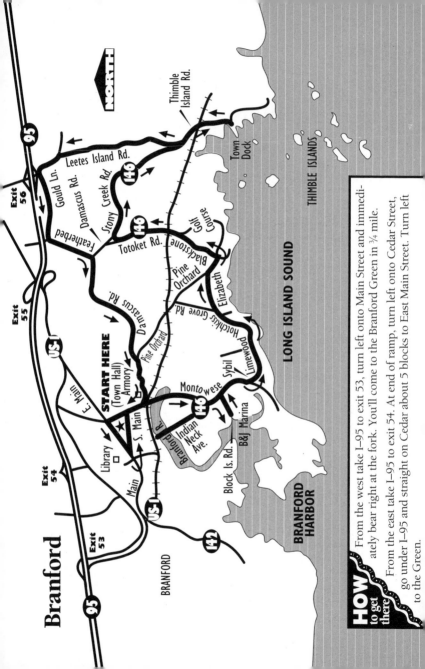

Branford

NORTH

95 — Exit 56
Exit 55
Exit 54
Exit 53

Leetes Island Rd.
Gould Ln.
Damascus Rd.
Stony Creek Rd.
Featherbed
146
146

Thimble Island Rd.

Totoket Rd.
Golf Course
Blackstone
Pine Orchard

Damascus Rd.
Pine Orchard

START HERE
(Town Hall)
Armory

E. Main
S. Main
Library
Main

US1
US1

Montowese
Indian Neck Ave.
Branford R.
Block Is. Rd.
B&J Marina
146

Hotchkiss Grove Rd.
Elizabeth
Sybil
Limewood

Town Dock

THIMBLE ISLANDS

LONG ISLAND SOUND

BRANFORD HARBOR

BRANFORD

146

HOW to get there

From the west take I–95 to exit 53, turn left onto Main Street and immediately bear right at the fork. You'll come to the Branford Green in ¾ mile.

From the east take I–95 to exit 54. At end of ramp, turn left onto Cedar Street, go under I–95 and straight on Cedar about 5 blocks to East Main Street. Turn left to the Green.

along the shore. As the road starts to turn inland be alert for the Connecticut sport, "fool the tourist by changing street names." You've been on Limewood Avenue, which becomes Hotchkiss Grove Road, which you leave as it goes left and inland at a Y where Second Avenue is on your right. Bear right on what is now Elizabeth Street (which may not be marked!) and ride past six side streets to where Pine Orchard Road takes over, coming down from your left. Turn right and go the short distance to where you turn left onto Blackstone Avenue, which is also Route 146. Ride up Blackstone, with the Pine Orchard Golf Club on your right and Young's Pond on the left, to the Y intersection with Totoket Road; bear left. Ride under the railroad tracks and up Totoket (Route 146) about ¾ mile to the Y intersection with what is called Damascus Road on the left and Stony Creek Road on the right. You are going to Stony Creek, so turn right. Stay on Stony Creek Road as it meanders for about 2 miles past the Wightwood School and the Trap Rock single-track railroad to the four-way intersection with Leetes Island and Thimble Island roads. Turn right and ride down Thimble Island Road into Stony Creek, a quirky waterfront village whose inhabitants call themselves "Creekers." Ride down to the town dock and give yourself a rare treat, a forty-five-minute cruise through the Thimble Islands. From June 1 through September 8 there are daily cruises departing at a quarter past the hour from 10:15 A.M. to 5:15 P.M. From May 4 through May 31 and September 9 to October 12, the cruises are on Friday, Saturday, and Sunday only. There are thirty-two tiny islands, all have fascinating histories.

As you ride back the way you came, stop and take a look inside the Stony Creek Puppet House Theater to see how the theater got its name. At the four-way intersection, ride straight ahead on Leetes Island Road to Gould Lane just before I–95. Turn left, ride to the T with Featherbed Lane, which comes from the other side of I–95, turn left, ride to the T with Damascus Road and turn right, following Damascus down to the Y where you join Pine Orchard Road, bearing right to Montowese, and a right turn for the ride back to the green.

If you're thirsty, you can get an old-fashioned ice cream soda at the Branford Candy Shop's 1939 soda fountain on Main Street across from the green before you leave town.

Chester–East Haddam

Number of miles:	14
Approximate pedaling time:	2 hours
Terrain:	fairly flat on the west side of the river, definitely hilly on the east side
Surface:	good
Things to see:	the Connecticut River, Gillette Castle, Goodspeed Opera House, Gelston House Restaurant, towns of Chester and East Haddam

There are many pluses on this ride: the five-minute ferry trip on the Chester-Hadlyme ferry, the Rhine River–like view from the terrace at Gillette Castle, the Victorian mood of the Goodspeed Opera House, the varied terrain, and, above all, the lively Connecticut River.

Park your car in Chester Center near the handsome stone building that stands at the principal intersection. (The building, incidentally, is *not* a courthouse; it is a package store!) Start by heading east on Route 148, crossing Route 154, to the Hadlyme Ferry. The ferry operates from April 1 to November 30 from 7:00 A.M. to 8:45 P.M. Cyclists ride for only 75 cents and don't have to wait in line. After crossing the river, proceed up the steep hill to the left for about a mile to Gillette Castle State Park. Be careful on this heavily traveled, narrow road. The castle is ½ mile from the park's entrance. It was built in the late nineteenth and early twentieth centuries by the actor William Gillette, who made his fame and fortune playing the role of Sherlock Holmes on stage for many years all over the United States. He designed his home and had it built atop 184 acres overlooking the wide and beautiful Connecticut River. Each of the twenty-four rooms

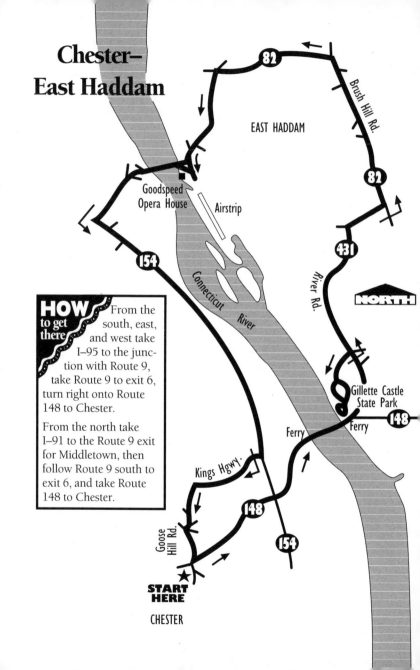

Chester–East Haddam

82

EAST HADDAM

Brush Hill Rd.

82

Goodspeed
Opera House

Airstrip

431

154

Connecticut River

River Rd.

NORTH

HOW
to get
there
From the south, east, and west take I–95 to the junction with Route 9, take Route 9 to exit 6, turn right onto Route 148 to Chester.

From the north take I–91 to the Route 9 exit for Middletown, then follow Route 9 south to exit 6, and take Route 148 to Chester.

Gillette Castle
State Park

148

Ferry   Ferry

Kings Hgwy.

148

154

Goose Hill Rd.

★ **START
HERE**

CHESTER

is unique. If you can, take the time to go through it. Admission is free.

Turn left as you leave the park. You will now have a very hilly ride to the intersection with Route 82 (Brush Hill Road), where you turn left. Continue bearing left on Route 82. In a little over a mile there will be a stop sign; turn sharply left (still on 82) and you will be exhilarated by the 1-mile downhill into the town of East Haddam. While here be sure to visit the Goodspeed Opera House, lovingly and authentically restored in the 1960s; and take time to browse the attractive shops that line the streets. Be sure to pull off the road and ride down, behind the Opera House, to the bank of the river for a picnic and to watch the small airplanes landing on the strip nearby or the passengers boarding cruise ships for outings on the river and to Long Island. (In the last half of the 1800s, steamboat traffic from New York to Hartford brought many fashionable people to the town.)

Upon leaving East Haddam, take the bridge over the river, riding on the solid area close to the railing. Turn left at the T intersection, complete with traffic light, of Routes 82 and 154 south. In about 3 miles, after passing Goose Hill Road on the right and the Susan Bates knitting needle factory on the left, you'll come to Kings Highway; turn right and go uphill to the T intersection with Goose Hill Road. Turn left. In about ½ mile bear left again, continuing on Goose Hill Road, which will take you downhill into Chester at the intersection where you left your car.

Essex

Number of miles:	13½
Approximate pedaling time:	2 hours
Terrain:	gentle to downright hilly
Surface:	good
Things to see:	Griswold Inn, the Connecticut River, several marinas, the Copper Beech Inn, Ivoryton Playhouse, and the Valley Railroad

Essex is one of the jewels in Connecticut's crown. It's a river town and mighty expensive to live in but a joy to visit. If you like sailboats or large power yachts—feast your eyes!

Begin by parking your car behind the Town Hall, just past the Route 9 overpass on Route 153 (West Avenue). Mount up and proceed downhill into Essex proper, passing the Pratt House and Smithy; bear around to the left, following the sign into Old Essex. Turn right at Main Street, and follow it, past the Griswold Inn, down to the river's edge. Here you will find a river full of large sailing yachts (boats this big are yachts!) and the Connecticut River Museum at Steamboat Dock, an 1878 steamboat warehouse open Tuesday through Sunday, 10:00 A.M. to 5:00 P.M.

Turn around and come up Main to Ferry Street; turn right. Ferry Street ends at the ferry slip (for a tiny ferry with fringe on top, which goes to the Essex Island Marina). After a look at all the dream boats, turn left on Pratt Street, head uphill to North Main Street, turn right, and within ½ mile you'll find a cemetery on your right. Go into the cemetery, down to the water's edge. This is a beautiful spot to rest.

Return to North Main Street and turn right. In about 1 mile North

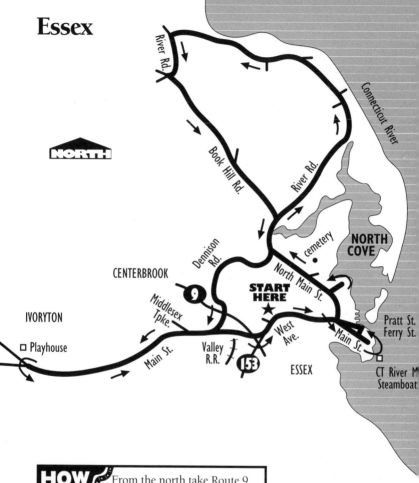

Essex

NORTH

River Rd.

Connecticut River

Book Hill Rd.

River Rd.

Dennison Rd.

cemetery

NORTH COVE

CENTERBROOK

North Main St.

START HERE ★

IVORYTON

Middlesex Tpke.

9

Main St.

Valley R.R.

153

West Ave.

Main St.

ESSEX

Pratt St.
Ferry St.

CT River M
Steamboat

□ Playhouse

HOW to get there From the north take Route 9 south to exit 3, follow the signs on Route 153 into Essex.

From the east take I–95 west to exit 69 to Route 9 to exit 3 and on into Essex.

From the west take I–95 to exit 65. Turn left onto Route 153 and follow it to Essex.

Main becomes River Road. After another 2 miles you'll come to a stop sign at the juncture of River Road and Book Hill Road. Make the 160-degree turn left onto Book Hill Road. It's a steep hill, but after a mile the road goes as steeply downhill for a fine, free ride for ½ mile, until the T intersection of Book Hill and River roads. Turn right onto River Road and ride ¼ mile to the intersection of Dennison Road. Turn 45 degrees right onto Dennison, and you are on the road to Ivoryton, about 3 miles from this point.

Dennison takes you over Route 9 and then to the little town of Centerbrook. At the intersection of Dennison and Middlesex Turnpike, turn right and follow the signs to Ivoryton. Middlesex Turnpike will soon bear almost 90 degrees right. Continue straight on what is now Main Street, past the renowned Copper Beech Inn, into Ivoryton.

Check out the Ivoryton Playhouse and the tiny square, then double back on Main Street, passing Dennison Road, bearing right on Middlesex Turnpike to the Valley Railroad, which is well worth a stop! Better yet, give it a couple of hours and ride the antique steam train to Deep River to board an authentic riverboat for an hour's cruise on one of America's most beautiful rivers, the Connecticut.

Continue on Middlesex Turnpike, downhill, under Route 9, and immediately left at the traffic light onto West Avenue. You are back in Essex, ⅓ mile from the Town Hall and your starting place.

Guilford

Number of miles:	20½
Approximate pedaling time:	2½ hours
Terrain:	mostly gentle, a couple of tough hills
Surface:	good
Things to see:	Guilford Green and harbor, Henry Whitfield House, Hyland House, Griswold House, Monastery of Our Lady of Grace

Guilford, one of Connecticut's shoreline towns, has more than one hundred houses built in the eighteenth century and the oldest stone house in the United States, plus one of the prettiest greens—as you will soon see. Begin in Guilford at the junction of I–95 and Route 77, where you can park in either of the two commuter parking lots on the north side of I–95. Ride south on Route 77. You are heading toward the Guilford Green and the sea. After about 1 mile, you'll come to the green. This is one of the loveliest commons in New England. It is flanked by a spired white Congregational church, stately houses, and quaint shops. At the green turn right onto Broad Street and then left on Whitfield Street, which will take you down to the Sound. In a mile you will see the striking Henry Whitfield House on the left. Built in 1639 with dense stone walls, a sixty-degree, sloping tiled roof, leaded windows, and twin chimneys, it is reputedly the oldest stone house in America. It is furnished with period pieces and is open to the public. It's a short ride to the house—for a long journey back in time, to early colonial days. To get to it, bear left at the Y with Old Whitfield and Whitfield and ride up to the house. When you're ready to leave turn left on Old Whitfield and then right onto Summer

Guilford

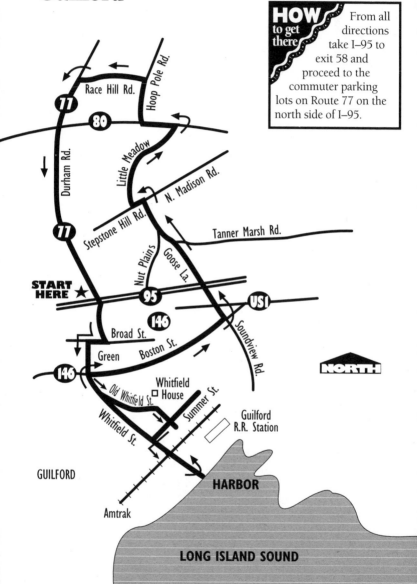

HOW to get there — From all directions take I–95 to exit 58 and proceed to the commuter parking lots on Route 77 on the north side of I–95.

Race Hill Rd.

Hoop Pole Rd.

77

80

Little Meadow

N. Madison Rd.

Durham Rd.

Stepstone Hill Rd.

Tanner Marsh Rd.

77

Nut Plains

Goose La.

START HERE ★

95

US1

146

Soundview Rd.

Broad St.

Green

Boston St.

NORTH

146

Whitfield House

Old Whitfield St.

Summer St.

Whitfield St.

Guilford R.R. Station

GUILFORD

Amtrak

HARBOR

LONG ISLAND SOUND

Street, which takes you the short distance back to Whitfield where a turn left will head you toward the harbor. Back in the present, ride over the railroad tracks for a sweeping view of the Sound and the reed-rich marshes, characteristic of the Connecticut shoreline. Proceed to the harbor past the Beecher House (1740). At the harbor there are three good restaurants to tempt you, or you can have a picnic sitting on the rocks at harborside.

On the return, ride up Whitfield back to the green. Turn right at the foot of the green onto Boston Street (it may not be marked). The Hyland House (1660) and the Griswold House (1735), both open to the public, are on Boston Street. Ride to Soundview Road. You are now approximately 9 miles from your starting point. Turn left, going under the turnpike.

Soundview becomes Goose Lane. In about a mile, Goose Lane turns left where Tanner Marsh Road comes in from the right. Continue on Goose Lane for about ½ mile to where Nut Plains Road comes in from the left. There is an old, small cemetery on the right; keep to the right. Goose Lane is now Nut Plains Road, which soon forms a T with Stepstone Hill Road (to the right this road is called North Madison Road).

Go left up very steep Stepstone Hill Road and turn right near the top of the hill onto Little Meadow Road. Now you'll have a downhill swing on Little Meadow Road all the way to Route 80. (Bear right at the fork formed by Little Meadow and Hoop Pole roads.) When you reach Route 80, turn left and go uphill about 7/10 mile to Hoop Pole Road. Turn right. After going uphill past ponds and woods, you'll come to Our Lady of Grace Monastery (Dominican nuns). Turn left here onto Race Hill Road. Turn left at the bottom of the hill onto Route 77 (Durham Road). When you come to the junction with Route 80, continue on Route 77, for about 4 miles, mostly downhill, to your starting place at Route 77 and I–95.

Killingworth

Number of miles:	14
Approximate pedaling time:	2 hours
Terrain:	more downhill than uphill
Surface:	good
Things to see:	Country Squire Inn and Antique Shop, several fine churches and houses, Chatfield Hollow State Park

For nineteen years, since the book was first published in 1976, the Killingworth ride ran counterclockwise: east on Route 80, north on 145, west on 148, and south on 81. The west leg on 148 was a 3½ mile uphill grind. For average recreational bicyclists, such as Jane Griffith and I were back then, it was a gut buster.

I confess that it never occurred to me to reverse it until an enthusiastic and astute bicyclist, Christopher Devine, wrote and asked the obvious question: Why not reverse the direction and turn that grinding uphill into a fast and refreshing downhill?

So here it is, clockwise and with the additional change of Roast Meat Hill Road instead of Route 81 for the left-hand leg, also recommended by Christopher Devine. Of course if you're a long-distance rider or racer, feel free to ride it the old way.

This is an out-in-the-country ride that takes you through no towns, no villages, just beautiful countryside. You can begin by parking your car or van or what-have-you in the Park-and-Ride lot on the northeast corner of Routes 80 and 81. When you're ready to roll, head east on Route 80 for 1 mile to Roast Meat Hill Road on the left. Turn left and head north. Roast Meat Hill is a lightly traveled country road, which takes you uphill—but not too steep—the 2½ miles to

Killingworth

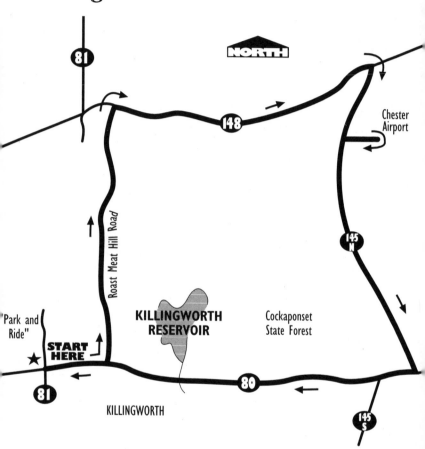

HOW to get there

From the south take I–95 to exit 63; head north on Route 81 to Route 80.

From the north take Route 9 out of Middletown to exit 9; head south on Route 81 to Route 80.

Route 148. Turn right and begin a fast, 3-mile descent to the junction with Route 145; turn right. Within ¾ mile there'll be a road to the left to the Chester Airport. Do go up and pay it a visit. There's a 1940s, relaxed, pre–WW II atmosphere about it. Also something of importance to those of us who are out on the road—rest rooms!

When you reach Route 80 turn right for the 4-mile ride back to the starting place. You'll be in the township of Deep River for the first half, passing Route 145 south and a lake on the left.

Route 145 is mostly downhill, and as you near the junction with Route 80, the tree-shaded road snakes left and right through a Hobbit-like glen; perhaps Orcs dwell in this part of the forest!

Before you head home or to the next ride, Guilford, perhaps, or Essex, ride or drive west on Route 80 to Chatfield Hollow State Park, which is only a mile from where you parked. It's a perfect spot to picnic and/or swim and enjoy the coolness of the hollow after your workout.

Madison–Hammonasset

Number of miles:	17
Approximate pedaling time:	2½ hours
Terrain:	flat to slightly hilly
Surface:	good
Things to see:	the shoreline town of Madison with its exceptional Congregational church, Hammonasset State Park

Madison is often called a bedroom town for New Haven, but only by those who don't live there. It not only is a beautiful New England small town but also has within its borders Hammonasset State Park, the largest beach in Connecticut—and a favorite place for walks along the beach in the spring, fall, and winter.

The best place to start from is the commuter Park-and-Ride lot on Goose Lane (exit 59 off I–95) in Guilford. When you're ready to ride, turn right from the parking lot, go under I–95 to the intersection with Route 1, and turn left. One mile into the ride brings you to the East River. Here there are marshes on both sides of the road, and you'll enjoy a lovely view of the sound. About ½ mile from the East River, turn left onto Wildwood Avenue, which takes you through the country part of Madison, fine in the summer and even better in the fall. The road snakes around to the right and forks; take the right fork. Your road becomes Green Hill. Soon you pass Nortontown Road and then another fork; bear right. The road starts uphill at this point, levels off as you pass Copse Road, and then goes briefly uphill again.

At the 4-mile point Green Hill crosses Route 79. Continue on Green Hill, which curves around and down to the intersection with Horse Pond Road. Turn right onto Horse Pond, which has a wide

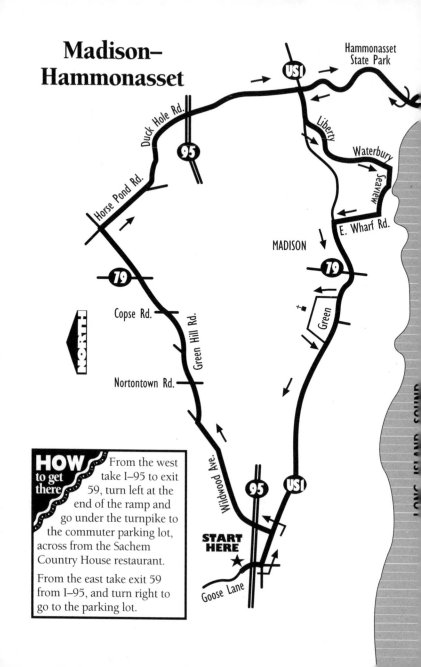

Madison–
Hammonasset

Hammonasset
State Park

US1

Duck Hole Rd.

95

Liberty

Waterbury

Seaview

Horse Pond Rd.

E. Wharf Rd.

MADISON

79

79

Copse Rd.

Green Hill Rd.

Green

NORTH

Nortontown Rd.

Wildwood Ave.

95

US1

LONG ISLAND SOUND

HOW
to get
there
From the west
take I–95 to exit
59, turn left at the
end of the ramp and
go under the turnpike to
the commuter parking lot,
across from the Sachem
Country House restaurant.

From the east take exit 59
from I–95, and turn right to
go to the parking lot.

START
HERE
★

Goose Lane

shoulder. Within 1½ miles Horse Pond goes off to the right; continue straight on your present road, which becomes Duck Hole Road. At the intersection of Duck Hole with Route 1, there is a traffic light at the bottom of a hill. Cross over and enter Hammonasset State Park. You will find 2 miles of sandy beach, complete with dressing and rest rooms and snack bars (open only in the summer), as well as a boardwalk—all part of a 919-acre state park. Lock your bikes and have a swim and/or a picnic or just a leisurely stroll along the beautiful, white sand beach.

Come back out to Route 1 and turn left. The road goes gently up and down, and at the bottom of the third hill there is a caution light. Turn left onto Liberty Street. At Waterbury Avenue turn left and ride down to the shore for an uncluttered view of the sound as you turn right onto Seaview. When you reach East Wharf Road, turn right. Soon East Wharf forms a T with Route 1. Turn left and go through the small but well-manicured shopping section.

After passing the intersection of Routes 79 and 1 (Main Street), you will come upon the green. Bear right and loop around the green, passing in front of the magnificent First Congregational Church, built in 1707. Return to Route 1 and continue on it past West Wharf Road and the cemetery. Return to Goose Lane in Guilford and your starting place.

New Haven–East Rock

Number of miles:	9
Approximate pedaling time:	1¼ hours
Terrain:	flat in the city, then up and down fabulous East Rock
Surface:	good
Things to see:	New Haven Green, New Haven Colony Historical Society, Peabody Museum, East Rock Park and THE VIEW, Lake Whitney, Edgerton Park

This is a spectacular 9-mile circuit from the New Haven Green to the summit of East Rock and back. You won't believe you did it until you reach the top of East Rock, 365 feet above the plain, and suddenly see the city and surrounding countryside, the harbor, and Long Island Sound below you! Note that the summit is closed from November 1 till April 1, *except* from 8:00 A.M.to 4:00 P.M. on Saturdays, Sundays, and holidays.

The ride begins at the corner of Elm and Church streets at the green. Head north on Church Street. In 2 blocks you will notice that Church changes its name to Whitney Avenue—it's a fine old New England custom.

At the corner of Sachem and Whitney, you'll pass the Peabody Museum of Natural History, which is well worth a long visit, and other buildings of Yale University. Proceed to Edwards Street. Take a right on Edwards and a left onto Livingston. At the corner of Cold Spring Street and Livingston, you will find yourself at College Woods, a part of East Rock Park. Proceed straight to East Rock Road. Turn right and cross the Mill River. Dead ahead you'll confront 365 feet of

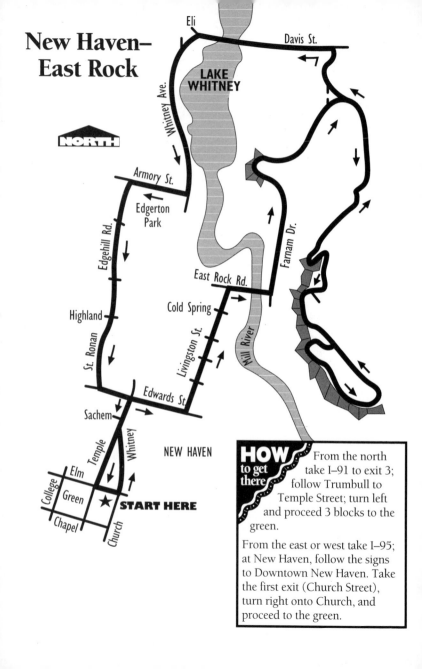

New Haven–East Rock

NORTH

Eli

Davis St.

LAKE WHITNEY

Whitney Ave.

Armory St.

Edgerton Park

Edgehill Rd.

Farnam Dr.

East Rock Rd.

Cold Spring

Highland

Livingston St.

St. Ronan

Mill River

Edwards St.

Sachem

Temple

Whitney

NEW HAVEN

Elm

College

Green

Church

Chapel

★ **START HERE**

HOW to get there

From the north take I–91 to exit 3; follow Trumbull to Temple Street; turn left and proceed 3 blocks to the green.

From the east or west take I–95; at New Haven, follow the signs to Downtown New Haven. Take the first exit (Church Street), turn right onto Church, and proceed to the green.

stone: the near-vertical face of East Rock. Turn left onto Farnam Drive to begin your gradual climb. Farnam Drive makes a long loop to the meadow on the north and then snakes its way to the summit, which has several great spots for picnicking.

The ride down is heavenly! Take the same route, bearing right after passing through the gate, then turning left when Farnam comes to a T at Davis Street. Cross the bridge over Lake Whitney, and bear left at the intersection formed by Eli and Davis streets. Ride a few yards up the hill to the traffic light on Whitney Avenue; turn left.

At the next traffic light turn right onto Armory Street. The property on the left, which resembles a fortification from Quebec, is, in fact, a storage facility of the New Haven Water Company. The little house on the corner (1799) was a boarding house for Eli Whitney's gun factory. Go 1 block to Edgehill Road and turn left. At number 145 Edgehill, on the left, there is a secret garden, Edgerton Park—a walled park of several rolling acres, which is open to all. There is also a mystery: Where is the mansion of the estate? Alas, it was destroyed at the stipulation of the donors in their will.

Edgehill becomes St. Ronan when you cross Highland. When St. Ronan forms a T with Edwards Street, turn left and go downhill to Whitney, where you turn right. Best to take the sidewalk here. Whitney forks at the minipark at Trumbull Street; bear right. Cross Elm and take a short tour of New Haven's picturesque green before returning to your car.

New Haven– Sleeping Giant

Number of miles:	25
Approximate pedaling time:	3½ hours
Terrain:	hilly
Surface:	mostly good, some rough spots
Things to see:	New Haven Green, Yale University, Sleeping Giant State Park, John Dickerman House, Quinnipiac College, Hamden

New Haven needs no introduction, but you may not be familiar with the Sleeping Giant. The best vantage point from which to see him is on I–91 heading north out of New Haven. As you approach exit 8, look ahead and to the left and there he is, sleeping on his back, about 2 miles long from his head to his feet!

Start your ride from College Street at the green. Go to the archway called Phelps Gate in the center of the block-long Yale University building, which flanks College Street. Ride through the arch and across the Old Campus to High Street. Turn right and go to Grove. (If the gate to the Old Campus is closed, go left on College to Chapel, then right 1 block to High and right to Grove.) This is the heart of the university. Turn left on Grove and curve past the gymnasium (largest in the world, per Mr. Guinness) to the traffic light. Be careful here. Bear right past Dixwell and Goffe, and turn right on Whalley Avenue.

Proceed out Whalley, which bears to the right 2⅖ miles from the start at the junction of Routes 243 and 63 (Whalley is 63). In another mile you will come to the Y intersection of 63 and 69; bear right onto 69. Within ½ mile you'll find yourself on a two-lane country road,

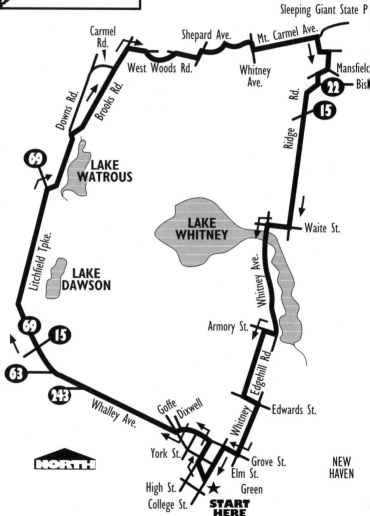

New Haven–
Sleeping Giant

HOW to get there

See Ride 26, New Haven–East Rock.

Sleeping Giant State P

Carmel Rd.

Shepard Ave.

Mt. Carmel Ave.

West Woods Rd.

Whitney Ave.

Mansfiel

22 Bis

Downs Rd.

Brooks Rd.

69

Ridge Rd.

15

LAKE WATROUS

LAKE WHITNEY

Waite St.

Litchfield Tpke.

LAKE DAWSON

Whitney Ave.

Armory St.

69 **15**

63

Edgehill Rd

243

Whalley Ave.

Goffe

Dixwell

Edwards St.

Whitney

York St.

Grove St.

Elm St.

NORTH

High St.

College St.

Green

START HERE

NEW HAVEN

which takes you uphill past farms and a lovely lake, Lake Dawson. A mile past the lake, as Route 69 (Litchfield Turnpike) goes left, turn right on Downs Road and then right onto Brooks Road. Ride down Brooks Road about 3 miles, passing Carmel Road on the left, to West Woods Road. Turn right on West Woods. At Choate, West Woods goes right and then loops gently to the left. At Shepard Avenue, go left for 1 block and then turn right back onto West Woods, which will now take you 1 mile to Whitney Avenue. Turn right onto Whitney, then left onto Mt. Carmel Avenue. On the right you will see the Jonathan Dickerman House, built in 1770. It is open on summer weekends and is worth visiting. On the left is Sleeping Giant State Park. There is a bike rack inside the entrance.

When leaving the park, proceed on Mt. Carmel past Quinnipiac College to Ridge Road; turn right. Ridge Road goes up and down for about 2 miles before leveling off. When you come to a T intersection, turn right, following Ridge Road as it goes up and over Route 22 and then bears gently to the left. Continue on Ridge Road for 3 miles to Waite Street, where you turn right, run downhill to Whitney Avenue, and turn left. Here is a stunning view of East Rock across Lake Whitney. You are about 4 miles from your starting point on the New Haven Green.

Follow Whitney Avenue to Armory Street across from the dam. Turn right, then go left on Edgehill Road. (If you're ready for a respite, turn into Edgerton Park on the left.) Follow Edgehill (which soon changes its name to St. Ronan) to Edwards Street, a T intersection. Turn left, go to Whitney once more, and turn right. At Grove Street, turn right, then turn left at College and back to your car.

New Haven–Lighthouse Point

Number of miles:	13
Approximate pedaling time:	2 hours
Terrain:	flat with several small hills
Surface:	good to excellent
Things to see:	New Haven Green, Morris Cove, Lighthouse Point Park, Pardee Morris House, Wooster Square

New Haven–Lighthouse Point was one of our first rides, and it's still a favorite. You'll get to see some interesting parts of New Haven, like the Wooster Square area, take a swim with a picnic (we're great on picnicking) at New Haven's only public beach, and finish with a ride on a beautifully restored carousel. Start at the New Haven Green, on the corner of Church and Elm streets. You can park your car at any spot around the green. Go east on Elm over the railroad tracks; bear right onto Olive Street. Continue on Olive about ½ mile until you come to Water Street; turn left. Go under the turnpike and over the drawbridge onto what is now Forbes Avenue. After 6 blocks, start up the hill, which spirals right, then left, and peaks at the junction with Woodward Avenue, the first stoplight (it may not be marked). Turn right; cross over I–95 and go straight on Woodward Avenue. After about a mile you'll come to Rayham Road (spelled Raynham at the upper end), the street after the caution light. Stop and take a look. Sitting at the top of the hill, you'll see a large Victorian mansion, just the width of Raynham Road. It's the Townshend Mansion, owned and occupied by the same family since 1840. In 1½ miles, Woodward and the water meet at Nathan Hale Park. Woodward Avenue turns inland here and ends as it runs into Townsend Avenue. Turn right and

New Haven–Lighthouse Point

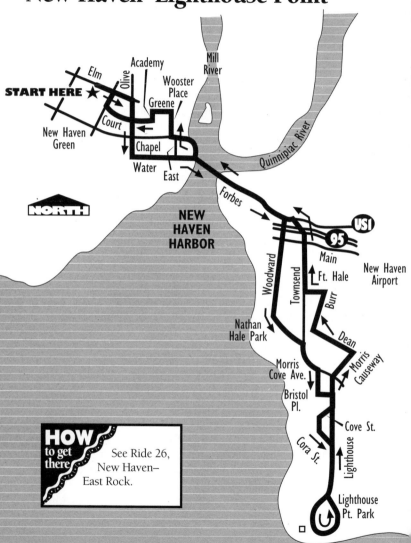

within ½ mile, you come to Morris Cove, where you'll have a fine view of New Haven Harbor. Turn right onto Morris Cove Avenue at the end of the cove. Turn left in ½ block when it ends at Bristol Place. Turn right at the intersection with Lighthouse and right again on Cove Street, then left on Cora Street, back to Lighthouse Avenue and the entrance to Lighthouse Point Park. Turn right into the park. It's ½ mile to the beach proper, a lovely beach with a bathhouse and an old-fashioned carousel full of lovingly restored wooden horses. Closed on Mondays only. Lighthouse Point also has the rare distinction of being one of the rest stops for monarch butterflies during their annual migration to central Mexico. During the last week of September and first week of October, the butterflies alight in the trees near the carousel to rest before flying (or is it fluttering?) on to Mexico.

From the park you return to Lighthouse Road, and within ½ mile, you will find the Pardee Morris House on the right, built in 1685 and open to the public from May 1 to November 1 on Saturdays and Sundays only from 11:30 A.M. to 4:00 P.M.

From the Morris House, continue downhill to Townsend Avenue. Cross Townsend onto the very short Morris Causeway to Dean Street; turn left. Continue to Burr Street; turn right and go to Fort Hale Road, the first street on the left past the airport terminal (which has a nifty restaurant, with restrooms, overlooking the runways). Turn left and ride uphill to Townsend Avenue where you turn right. Soon you will cross Main Street and I–95. Turn left at the next street, Forbes Avenue. Ride past Woodward, downhill, reversing your outbound track, going over the drawbridge to a right-hand turn at East Street, the first after crossing the bridge. Turn left at the next light, onto Chapel Street. At Wooster Place turn right and make a circuit of Wooster Park, with a left on Greene and a left on Academy. Midway down Academy, turn right onto Court, a short pedestrian/bicycle-only street between Academy and Olive. Continue across Olive, over the railroad, past State and Orange, using the sidewalk since the street is one way in the opposite direction, to Church Street and the New Haven Green.

Old Saybrook

Number of miles:	12
Approximate pedaling time:	1¼ hours
Terrain:	flat
Surface:	good
Things to see:	eighteenth-century houses, Connecticut River, Long Island Sound, Old Saybrook, Fenwick, the Castle Inn at Cornfield Point

This ride takes you on a tour of Old Saybrook's considerable waterfront—North Cove, Saybrook Point, Lynde Point, and Cornfield Point—with stops in between, including a soda or ice cream cone at a soda fountain that's been serving them since 1896! Park at any convenient spot on Main Street and ride south on Main (Route 154). When you reach the large Congregational church at the end of the shopping area, note on your right the James Gallery and Soda Fountain with its large gold mortar and pestle frieze, above the second story windows. It was built in 1790 and operated as a pharmacy from 1877 until 1917 by one Peter Lane. In 1917, Lane turned the pharmacy over to his sister-in-law, Ana James, the first black woman pharmacist in Connecticut, who ran it as James Pharmacy until 1967. The soda fountain dates back to 1896—don't pass it by!

At the large arrow traffic sign bear left. (Route 154 is now called College Street.) When you come to North Cove Road, turn left and follow it to the shore of North Cove, a large, protected anchorage, chock-full of sailboats large and small—mostly large—swinging at their moorings. Continue around on Cromwell Place, which leads

Old Saybrook

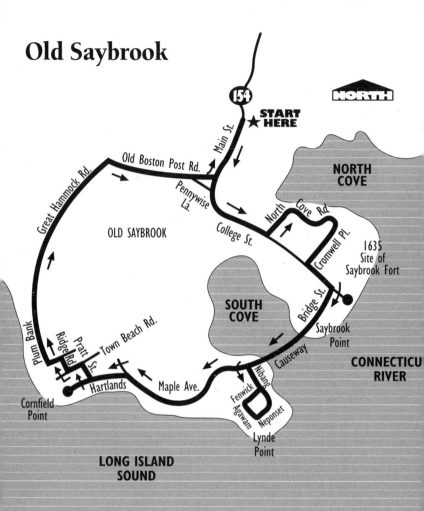

154

★ START HERE

NORTH

Main St.

Old Boston Post Rd.

Great Hammock Rd.

Pennywise La.

OLD SAYBROOK

College St.

North Cove Rd.

NORTH COVE

Cromwell Pl.

1635 Site of Saybrook Fort

Bridge St.

SOUTH COVE

Saybrook Point

Causeway

CONNECTICUT RIVER

Plum Bank

Ridge Rd.

Pratt St.

Town Beach Rd.

Hartlands

Maple Ave.

Nibang

Fenwick

Agawam

Neponset

Cornfield Point

Lynde Point

LONG ISLAND SOUND

HOW to get there From the north take Route 9 to I–95, go west to exit 67, and follow Route 154 into Old Saybrook.

From the east take I–95 to exit 67, turn left, and go straight to East Main Street.

you back to College Street. Turn left onto College Street and follow it down to the riverside. There is a new marina as well as an inn on the right and several restaurants on the left. A picnic lunch can be enjoyed on the quay. An even better spot would be the park on the left just before the river, Fort Saybrook Monument Park (which has a public rest room).

When you are ready, return to College Street, turn left on what is now Bridge Street, and cross the causeway over South Cove. This is narrow, so ride carefully. The road is now called Maple Avenue. Turn left on the other side onto Nibang Avenue and take a mile-long circuit of Lynde Point. Back on Maple Avenue, turn left and you will soon find yourself riding beside Long Island Sound.

In the distance, you will see what appears to be a large stone mansion. To get to it, turn left on Hartlands Drive, between two stone pillars. Continue until you get to the Castle Inn, built in 1906 to rival the grandeur of Newport. Here you can get a room, a drink, or a meal.

When you leave the inn, turn left on Pratt Street, left on Town Beach Road, and immediately right on Ridge Road. In 2 blocks, you'll be back on Route 154, now called Plum Bank Road. It continues along the Sound, slowly swings inland, crosses Back River, and becomes Great Hammock Road. About 1½ miles from the inn, Great Hammock Road forms a T with the Old Boston Post Road. Turn right here and return to Main Street ⁷⁄₁₀ mile away.

Mystic–Stonington

Number of miles:	14½
Approximate pedaling time:	2 hours
Terrain:	generally flat, three hills
Surface:	good to only fair in spots; good shoulders where needed
Things to see:	Mystic, Mystic Seaport Museum, Stonington, Old Stone Lighthouse, Mystic Marinelife Aquarium

There are so many things to see on this ride that you just may have to come back and do it again. Start from the south (second) parking lot of Mystic Seaport Museum, just across from its entrance. Mount up and turn left onto Main Street. Turn immediately right on Isham Street. Ride the brief block to the Mystic River and turn left onto Bay Street. When Bay forms a T with Holmes Street, turn right. At the stop sign, turn left on East Main Street, then turn right at the Civil War Memorial onto Route 1. *Note:* If traffic is backed up in the right lane on Holmes waiting for the drawbridge over on the right, go around the traffic to East Main.

Stonington is 4 miles away. In about 3 miles, St. Mary's Cemetery will be on your right. Make a loop through it and turn right, back onto Route 1. Then turn right again on Route 1A (Water Street) toward Stonington Village.

Turn left on Trumbull Avenue. You will soon come to a stop sign at the foot of the only bridge over the railroad tracks; turn right to go over the bridge, then turn left onto Water Street, and begin the ride down to Stonington Point. The whole town is rich with eighteenth-century buildings, so you'll probably want to explore it thoroughly.

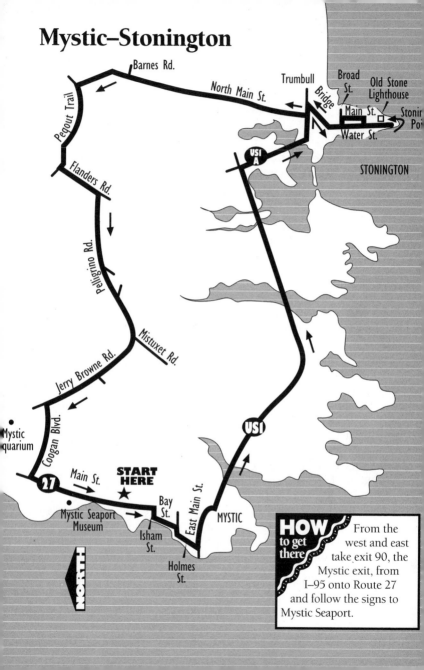

Mystic–Stonington

Barnes Rd.

Pequot Trail

North Main St.

Trumbull

Bridge

Broad St.

Old Stone Lighthouse

Main St.

Water St.

Stonir Poi

Flanders Rd.

USI A

STONINGTON

Pelligrino Rd.

Mistuxet Rd.

Jerry Browne Rd.

USI

Coogan Blvd.

Mystic quarium

27

Main St.

START HERE

East Main St.

Bay St.

Mystic Seaport Museum

Isham St.

Holmes St.

MYSTIC

NORTH

HOW to get there From the west and east take exit 90, the Mystic exit, from I–95 onto Route 27 and follow the signs to Mystic Seaport.

Just before the end of Water Street, the Old Stone Lighthouse Museum is on the left. Don't pass it by! Inside you will see, among many other things, what actually caused "the rocket's red glare" in our national anthem. The museum is open May through October, Wednesday through Sunday afternoons from 1:00 to 4:00. Here you are at the halfway point of the ride.

Proceed back up Water Street until you spot the sign that directs all traffic to the right around a tiny park. Turn right and then left onto Main Street. Notice the Old Custom House and the Portuguese Holy Ghost Society, a reminder of the Portuguese fishermen who settled in Stonington and still ply their dangerous calling from her docks. In these days of automated food factories and huge floating factory "fishing" ships, it's good to discover that men still go down to the sea in small boats to bring us fish and clams and oysters. Turn left on Broad Street and then right on Water Street to go back over the bridge. On the other side of the bridge, take an immediate left onto Trumbull and then a right onto North Main Street, which quickly becomes a country road. Then 2½ miles after your turn onto North Main Street, you'll come to a T intersection with Pequot Trail; turn left. After you see the "Road Church" on your left and just before the road goes over the turnpike, turn left onto Flanders Road (it may not be marked). In ³/₁₀ mile, turn right onto Pelligrino Road and go uphill. Continue on Pelligrino when Montauk Avenue comes in from the left. After the stop sign, just past Deans Mill Road, continue straight. Pelligrino Road becomes Jerry Browne Road at the point where Mistuxet comes in from the left. Continue on Jerry Browne Road uphill and down. Turn left onto Coogan Boulevard just before going under the turnpike. Coogan goes past the Mystic Marinelife Aquarium and the Old Mystic Village Shopping Center. Coogan makes a T at Route 27 at a busy intersection in a snarl of motels and gas stations. Turn left and head back to Mystic Seaport.

North Lyme

Number of miles:	12½
Approximate pedaling time:	1½ hours
Terrain:	definitely hilly
Surface:	fair
Things to see:	lovely country throughout, Eight Mile River, Hamburg, North Lyme

This has always been one of the most popular rides because of the beautiful countryside and the thrilling downhill runs. The best place to park your vehicle is on the side road off Route 156 that is to the right just before the large sign, NEHANTIC STATE FOREST 800 FEET.

Mount up and turn right onto Route 156. Proceed uphill; at the crest you will enjoy a scene of rolling hills and pastures. After a whopping downhill, a brief uphill will deliver you to the town of Hamburg, which borders the Eight Mile River. Soon after you pass a Congregational church, the road forks; take the left fork, Old Hamburg Road, down to the river's edge. When the road comes to a T, turn right. After turning you'll notice a good place to picnic at the riverside on your left, near the "Pont D'Avignon".

When you return to Route 156, turn left. The road follows the Eight Mile River for a time, meandering and going up and down. Just after you cross Beaver Brook, turn right onto Beaver Brook Road. For nearly 3 miles go along this two-lane country road, passing farms and handsome country houses. You will pass a road coming in from the right and then arrive at the intersection of Beaver Brook, Gungy (on the left), and Grassy Hill roads. Turn right onto Grassy Hill Road. You pass through a beautiful forest here whose dappled light makes this a perfect ride for a summer evening. When you come out of the woods,

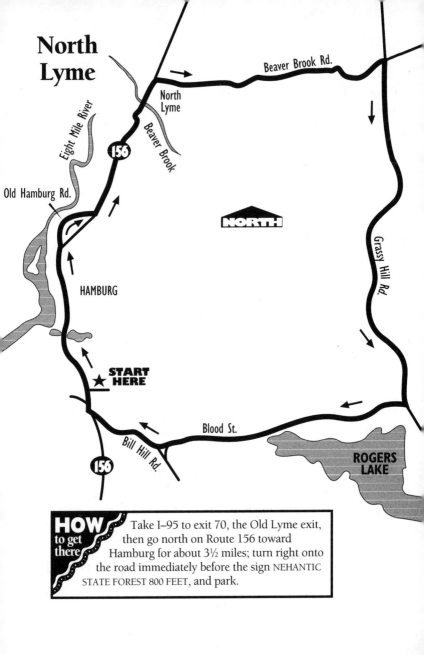

North Lyme

Beaver Brook Rd.

North Lyme

Eight Mile River

156

Beaver Brook

Old Hamburg Rd.

NORTH

HAMBURG

Grassy Hill Rd.

START HERE

Blood St.

Bill Hill Rd.

156

ROGERS LAKE

HOW to get there — Take I–95 to exit 70, the Old Lyme exit, then go north on Route 156 toward Hamburg for about 3½ miles; turn right onto the road immediately before the sign NEHANTIC STATE FOREST 800 FEET, and park.

the hill crests yielding a spacious view and a surprising field of ferns on the right. The Congregational church is set high on the hill to your left. A settled area follows this scene, and there are some steep downhills to the point where you turn off Grassy Hill Road.

Turn right at Blood Street, which T's into Grassy Hill Road. (If you are ready for a picnic at this time, continue straight on Grassy Hill Road a short distance to where Rogers Lake is close to the road. There you'll find picnic tables.) Blood Street borders Rogers Lake. This stretch is a rather densely populated resort area where there are a couple of steep hills. In about $1\frac{1}{2}$ miles bear right at the fork and go right again when the road forms a T with Bill Hill Road, just a few feet from the fork. Continue to the right as Bill Hill Road returns you to Route 156. Turn right when you reach 156, and in $\frac{1}{5}$ mile you will be back at your starting place.

Waterford–New London

Number of miles:	13¾
Approximate pedaling time:	1¾ hours
Terrain:	mostly flat, a couple of steep hills
Surface:	only fair in Waterford, good in New London
Things to see:	Atlantic Ocean, Thames River and New London Harbor, Harkness Memorial State Park, Ocean Beach Park

This circuit of Waterford and the western shore of New London harbor will show you many things and give you a choice of many things to do in only 13¾ miles. The best place to start from is the town hall parking lot on the right side of Route 156, just west of the junction of Routes 1 and 156 in Waterford. (The renovated town hall has nice rest rooms.)

Proceed west on 156 about ½ mile to Great Neck Road (Route 213), where you turn left. Great Neck narrows, so use the sidewalk on this stretch. Just before Great Neck swings to the left and down toward the Harkness Estate, you'll catch your first glimpse of the ocean. About 3½ miles into the ride, you reach the entrance to Harkness Memorial State Park. We recommend a stop here to visit the Newport-style mansion, with its enormous lawns and beautiful gardens.

Return to Route 213 and turn right, following signs to New London. At the first stop sign, turn right. At the next stop sign, turn left. (The O'Neill Theater is on the right.) Turn right when the road makes a **T** at Niles Hill Road. Go up Niles Hill. At the traffic light turn right onto Ocean Avenue, a **T** intersection, following the signs to

Waterford–New London

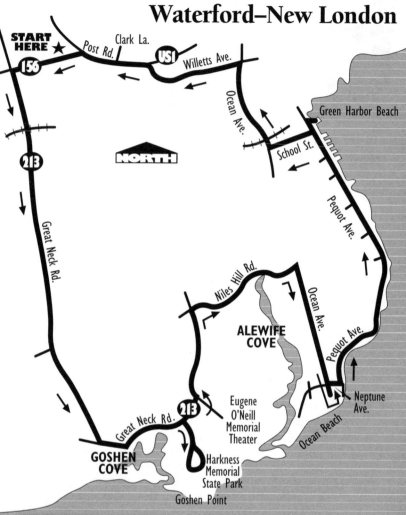

START HERE ★

156

Post Rd.   Clark La.   US1   Willetts Ave.

213

Great Neck Rd.

Ocean Ave.

Green Harbor Beach

School St.

Pequot Ave.

NORTH

Niles Hill Rd.

ALEWIFE COVE

Ocean Ave.

Pequot Ave.

Neptune Ave.

Great Neck Rd.   213

Eugene O'Neill Memorial Theater

GOSHEN COVE

Harkness Memorial State Park

Ocean Beach

Goshen Point

HOW to get there From the east or west take I–95 to exit 75, then go east on Route 1 (Boston Post Road) 4.8 miles, past three traffic lights to the fourth light at the junction of Route 1 and Route 156 west; turn right onto Route 156 and turn into the parking lot of the town hall.

Ocean Beach Park. Ocean Avenue is broad but very busy in the summer. When you reach Neptune Avenue, go straight ahead on Ocean Avenue, ignore the sign ONE WAY DON'T ENTER, and go through the pedestrian gate. There's no charge to "park" your bike—just be sure you lock it with a kryptonite lock to something fastened to the ground and where you can keep an eye on it! The parking lot at the end of Neptune Avenue is for motorized vehicles only.

Ocean Beach Park has a wide beach, well-maintained boardwalk, rides, restaurants, arcade, miniature golf, and water slide. With its view of the ocean, it's a good place for lingering over lunch.

Return to Neptune Avenue, turn right, cross Ocean Avenue, and then left onto Pequot Avenue. (Pequot is Mott Avenue to the right of Neptune.) You will enjoy an unobstructed view of New London's outer harbor as you ride along Pequot. As you approach downtown New London, you'll enter an area featuring small marinas, restaurants, and Monte Cristo Cottage, the boyhood home of Eugene O'Neill, and the setting for *Ah, Wilderness* and *Long Day's Journey into Night.* It's now a museum at 325 Pequot Avenue, about six houses before Thames Street. It is open Monday through Friday from 1:00 to 4:00 P.M. A photograph of it is on page 124.

At School Street, turn left and climb back up to Ocean Avenue; turn right. In less than a mile, you'll come to Willetts Avenue. Turn left up a gentle incline, then downhill to Route 1, where there is a traffic light. Make your left-hand turn carefully onto this busy highway. At Clark Lane and the next traffic light, be alert again. Go straight ahead, getting into the left lane so that you can turn forty-five degrees to the left onto Route 156 west, and return to the parking lot just beyond the intersection.

Combination Ride 33

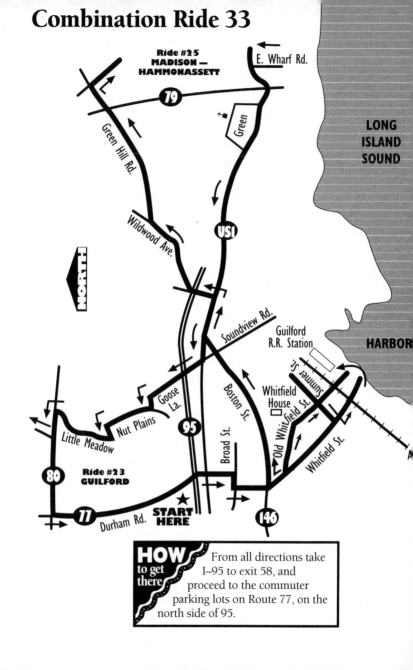

Ride #25
MADISON —
HAMMONASSETT

E. Wharf Rd.

79

Green

LONG
ISLAND
SOUND

Green Hill Rd.

Wildwood Ave.

US1

NORTH

Soundview Rd.

Guilford
R.R. Station

HARBOR

Whitfield
House

Summer St.

Goose La.

Boston St.

Whitfield St.

Old Whitfield St.

Nut Plains

Little Meadow

95

Broad St.

Whitfield St.

80

Ride #23
GUILFORD

77

Durham Rd.

★ START
HERE

146

HOW to get there — From all directions take I–95 to exit 58, and proceed to the commuter parking lots on Route 77, on the north side of 95.

Combination:
Guilford and Madison–Hammonasset

Number of miles:	38
Approximate pedaling time:	4 hours
Terrain:	mostly flat; a couple of steep hills and two long downhills
Surface:	good
Things to see:	Guilford Green and harbor, Henry Whitfield House, Hammonasset State Park

Here you have an opportunity to combine race training (if such is your pleasure) and sight-seeing. There are a couple of hills that offer a challenge, some fascinating sights along the way, and 2 miles of sand and sun at Hammonasset—all in 38 miles of bicycling!

Start at the commuter parking lot on Route 77, just north of I–95 in Guilford, where you can park in either of the two commuter parking lots on the north side of I-95. Follow the directions in Ride No. 23, Guilford, down 77 to the harbor.

When you return up Whitfield, turn right on Boston Street. When you reach Soundview Road, don't turn left; continue straight for the short distance to the T with Route 1, where you bear right and continue on Ride No. 25, Madison–Hammonasset (see page 97).

When you get to the end of this 17-mile ride, at Goose Lane on the north side of I–95, continue straight up Goose Lane and do the second half of the Guilford ride. This will take you on a jaunt through the North Guilford countryside, past Route 80 and then back down 77 to your starting place. This 38-mile circuit gives you a nice workout and the reward of a 4-mile downhill at the end.

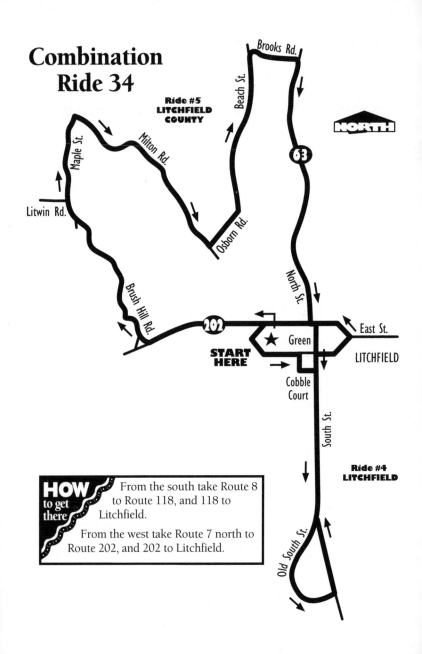

Combination:
Litchfield and Litchfield County

Number of miles:	16
Approximate pedaling time:	1½ to 2 hours
Terrain:	flat in town, mostly hilly out of town
Surface:	good
Things to see:	the handsome eighteenth-century houses of Litchfield, the superb Connecticut farmland and woods that surround it

The last leg of the Litchfield County Ride No. 5 is also the last one of the Litchfield Ride No.4, so you can either begin with Litchfield County and finish with the first half of Litchfield, or you can begin with Litchfield and as you come back around the green continue west on Route 202 onto the Litchfield County ride.

Follow the directions in the book for each ride.

Combination Ride 35

Ride #27
**NEW HAVEN-
SLEEPING GIANT**

Downs Rd.

Litchfield Tpke.

NORTH

69
15
63
243

Whalley

Goffe

Dixwell

Grove

Tower Pky.

Elm

College

START HERE

Temple

Church

Chapel

Court

Water

Temple

Armory

Edgehill

St. Ronan

Edwards

Whitney Ave.

Livingston

Whitney Ave.

Olive St.

Greene

Wooster Pl.

East St.

Mill River

Ride #26
NEW HAVEN-EAST ROCK

Forbes

HARBOR

Ride #28
**NEW HAVEN-
LIGHTHOUSE
POINT**

HOW
to get
there
Take I–95 to
New Haven
and get off at the
Church Street
(DOWNTOWN NEW
HAVEN) exit; turn right
onto Church, proceed to the
New Haven Green and park
in the area.

Combination:
New Haven–East Rock, Lighthouse Point, and Sleeping Giant

Number of miles:	47
Approximate pedaling time:	5 hours
Terrain:	flat in the city, a steep hill to East Rock summit, a long hill in the first half of the ride to Sleeping Giant
Surface:	good
Things to see:	New Haven, East Rock and its view, Wooster Square, Lighthouse Park, Sleeping Giant State Park

This combination makes a good race-training ride, with its 47 miles of varied terrain, flat city streets with traffic to contend with, steep sprint to the summit of East Rock, and long endurance uphill through the countryside.

The ride has the shape of a three-leaf clover: the stem is rooted in the New Haven Green, with the first leaf curving out to the north to East Rock Park and back; the second leaf reaches out to the northwest, then east to Sleeping Giant State Park, and back to the green in New Haven; and the third leaf stretches east to the beach at Lighthouse Point and back through Wooster Square.

Start from the green and head north on Church Street, following the directions in Ride No. 26, New Haven–East Rock, for the 9 miles to the Rock and back. Next, take off for Sleeping Giant from College Street to High to Grove and over to Whalley, following the instructions in ride No. 27, New Haven–Sleeping Giant.

When you return to the center of town after this 25-mile stretch, you might be ready for a swim, so head down Elm Street, following the New Haven–Lighthouse Point route (Ride No. 28) to the beach by the New Haven harbor breakwater. When you are completely refreshed, follow the map and directions back to the starting point.

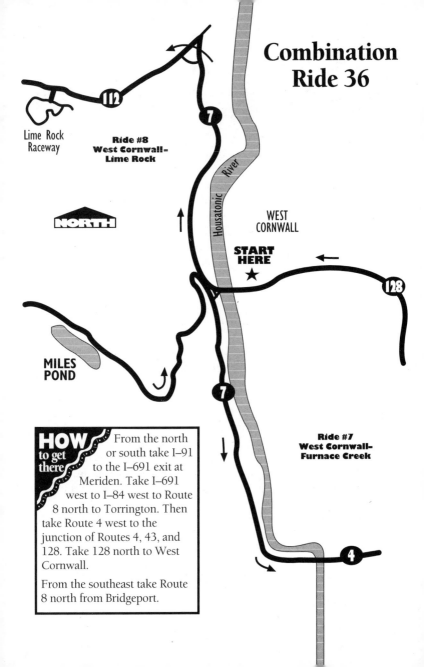

Combination Ride 36

112

Lime Rock Raceway

**Ride #8
West Cornwall–
Lime Rock**

7

Housatonic River

NORTH

WEST CORNWALL

START HERE
★

128

MILES POND

7

**Ride #7
West Cornwall–
Furnace Creek**

HOW to get there From the north or south take I–91 to the I–691 exit at Meriden. Take I–691 west to I–84 west to Route 8 north to Torrington. Then take Route 4 west to the junction of Routes 4, 43, and 128. Take 128 north to West Cornwall.

From the southeast take Route 8 north from Bridgeport.

4

Combination:
West Cornwall–Furnace Creek and West Cornwall–Lime Rock

Number of miles:	26
Approximate pedaling time:	3½ hours
Terrain:	definitely hilly but with several fine downhills
Surface:	good
Things to see:	an 1837 covered bridge (see and use), the hillside village of West Cornwall, Housatonic River, Furnace Creek, Lime Rock Raceway, the wildlife sanctuary, the splendor of northwest Connecticut's mountains and forests

Since both rides start from West Cornwall, you can begin with either one. I would suggest doing Ride No. 8, Lime Rock, first, for then you can continue with No. 7, Furnace Creek, without going through West Cornwall.

The best place to park is in the small post office lot on the right side of the street facing the river. When you are ready to ride, go over the river through the one-lane covered bridge and turn right if you choose to do Lime Rock first, or left if you have opted for Furnace Creek first. Both rides end with a fine and fitting downhill.

Follow the directions in the book for each ride, and when you're back in West Cornwall you can relax at that fine little restaurant that overlooks the creek.

Bicycle Shops in Connecticut

Al's Ordinary Bike Shop,
21 Furnace Street,
Danielson;
(860) 774-1660.
Repairs and sales.

Bicycle Barn,
1209 Poquonnock Road,
Groton;
(860) 448-2984.
Repairs and sales.

Bicycle Center,
612 Federal Road,
Brookfield;
(203) 775-7083.
Repairs and sales.

Bicycle Post,
310 Flander's Road Rear,
East Lyme;
(860) 739-6181.
Repairs and sales.

Bicycles East,
2333 Main Street,
Glastonbury;
(860) 659-0114.
Repairs and sales.

Bicycles of Danbury,
48 Pandanaram Road,
Danbury;
(203) 791-1250.
Repairs and sales.

Bike Doctor & Sports Center,
97 Church Street,
Canaan;
(860) 824-5577.

Bike Express of New Milford,
73 Bridge Street,
New Milford;
(860) 354-1466.
Repairs and sales.

Bike Express,
76 West Street,
Danbury;
(203) 792-5460.
Repairs and sales.

Bike Shop,
681 Main Street,
Manchester;
(860) 647-1027.
Repairs and sales.

Bloomfield Bicycle & Repair,
5 Seneca Road,
Bloomfield;
(860) 242-9884.
Repairs and sales.

Branford Bike,
1074 Main Street,
Branford;
(203) 488-0482.
Repairs and sales.

Clarke Cycles,
4 Essex Plaza,
Essex;
(860) 767-2405.
Repairs, sales, and rentals.

Cycle & Sport,
17 East Main Street,
Clinton;
(860) 669-5228.
Repairs and sales.

Cycle Loft,
25 Commons Drive,
Litchfield;
(860) 567-1713.
Repairs, sales, and rentals
(mountain bikes only).

Cycles of Madison,
698 Boston Post Road,
Madison;
(203) 245-8735.
Repairs, sales, and rentals
(hybrids only).

Dave's Cycle & Fitness Center,
78 Valley Road,
Cos Cob;
(203) 661-7736.
Repairs, sales, and rentals.

Don's Cycle Shop,
1964 Post Road,
Fairfield;
(203) 255-4079.
Repairs, sales, and rentals.

Farmington Bicycle Shop,
222 Main Street,
Farmington;
(860) 677-2453.
Repairs and sales.

Farr's
2 Main Street,
Manchester;
(860) 643-7111.
Repairs and sales.

Greenwich Bicycles,
40 West Putnam Avenue,
Greenwich;
(203) 869-4141.
Repairs, sales, and rentals.

Groton Schwinn Cyclery,
1360 Route 184,
Groton;
(860) 445-6745.
Repairs and sales.

Jules Bicycle Shoppe of Darien,
340 Heights Road,
Noroton Heights.
Repairs and sales.

Manchester Cycle Shop,
178 Middle Turnpike West,
Manchester;
(860) 649-2098.
Repairs and sales.

Meriden Bicycle Center,
294 East Main Street;
Meriden
(203) 238-2453.
Repairs and sales.

Mystic Cycle Center,
42 Williams Avenue,
Mystic;
(860) 572-7433.
Repairs, sales, and rentals
(hybrid and mountain bikes
only).

New Canaan Cyclery,
94 Park Street,
New Canaan;
(203) 966-2399.
Repairs and sales.

Newington Bicycle &
Repair Shop,
1030 Main Street,
Newington;
(860) 667-0857.
Repairs and sales.

North Haven Bicycle Center,
476 Washington Avenue,
North Haven;
(203) 239-7789.
Repairs and sales.

Pedal and Pump,
51 Tokeneke Road,
Darien;
(203) 655-2600.
Repairs and sales.

Pedal Power Bicycle & Repair,
500 Main Street,
Middletown;
(860) 347-3776.
Repairs and sales.

Pete's Cycles & Stoves,
934 Boston Post Road #D,
Guilford;
(203) 453-3544.
Repairs and sales.

Pig Iron Bicycle Works,
38 Addison Road,
Glastonbury;
(860) 659-8808.
Repairs and sales.

Rat's Bicycle Shop of Durham,
63 Main Street,
Durham;
(860) 349-8800.
Repairs and sales.

Spoke & Wheel Bike Shop,
2355 East Main Street,
Bridgeport;
(203) 384-8779.
Repairs and sales.

T C Cycle,
115 South Main Street,
Newton;
(203) 426-9111.
Repairs and sales.

Valley Bicycle Shop,
10 Hartford Avenue,
Granby;
(860) 653-6545.
Repairs, sales, and rentals.

Wayfarer Bicycle,
120 Ocean Avenue,
New London;
(860) 443-8250.
Repairs and sales.

World of Bikes,
317 South Main Street,
Newtown;
(203) 426-3335.
Repairs and sales.

Zane's Cycle,
105 North Main Street,
Branford;
(203) 488-3244.
Repairs, sales, and rentals.

About the Author

Edwin Mullen is a "Clamdigger." He qualified for that title by being born on City Island, a tiny island that sits just off the coast of the Bronx borough of New York City. Drafted into the army at age eighteen, he survived a brief stint as a twin-engine bomber pilot in Italy.

He has been an actor, producer, and purchasing agent for Yale University and now, contentedly retired from the latter, a freelance writer and actor, working for himself and his readers. Edwin Mullen has also written *Short Bike Rides™ on Cape Cod, Nantucket, and The Vineyard.*